Cooking Light

DINNERTIME SURVIVAL GUIDE

Cooking Light
DINNERTIME SURVIVAL GUIDE

Feed Your Family. Save Your Sanity.

SALLY KUZEMCHAK, MS, RD
Kid Wrangler. Mealtime Heroine. Nutrition Whiz.

Oxmoor
House.

Solve Your 10 Toughest
DINNERTIME DILEMMAS

A LOVE/HATE RELATIONSHIP

That's what I have with the idea of making dinner. I love watching my kids dig in to something I've just made. I love feeling good about what's on their plates. I love the thrill of finding a new recipe that garners smiles from everyone. And I love sitting around the table as a family.

But I hate all the stuff that makes dinner so hard to pull off. Like 25-minute windows between work and sports practices in which to cook and serve a meal for four. Or the rejection kids bestow on meals based solely on an innocent sprinkling of parsley.

BELIEVE IT! KIDS LOVE EATING AT HOME

In honor of Mother's Day, my son's preschool teachers asked this question: "What do you love about your mom?" The responses were: "She's pretty" or "She takes me places." Another said, "Her dress is soft." My Sam's response: "She makes dinner every night."

Sam is frequently the toughest customer at our house. He's not above a dinner strike or declaring a meal unacceptable before he's even seen it. Yet he loves me because I make those dinners just about every night. It's also possible that he couldn't think of anything else to say. Either way, I'll take it.

Getting dinner on the table isn't easy, even if you *like* to cook. Just because you *like* to cook doesn't necessarily mean you *want* to—or that you enjoy it while simultaneously reviewing spelling words and fielding an after-hours work call.

A NEVER-ENDING ASSIGNMENT

I remember when I got my first editorial job out of college. After my first day, I came home and collapsed onto my bed, exhausted—and totally exhilarated, until I realized: I had to go to work again tomorrow. And the next day and the day after that. It seemed to stretch into eternity.

DEDICATION

For my sons, Henry and Sam, and my husband, Joel, the three guys around my dinner table every night. I love you.

Math Worksheet

9/18/13

Score: _____
Date: _____
Name: Henry

$$\begin{array}{r} 36 \\ + 31 \\ \hline 67 \end{array}$$

$$\begin{array}{r} 49 \\ + 4 \\ \hline 85 \end{array}$$

$$\begin{array}{r} 35 \\ + 10 \\ \hline 45 \end{array}$$

$$\begin{array}{r} 33 \\ + 42 \\ \hline \end{array}$$

$$\begin{array}{r} 17 \\ + 36 \\ \hline \end{array}$$

Sometimes making dinner feels the same way. You spend time putting together a meal. And when it's all over, it hits you that this gig doesn't end today. It's the feeling that prompted my friend, Kelly, to post my favorite Facebook status update of all time: "These people have to be fed every day. EVERY DAY. I am so over it."

And yet there's deep satisfaction from knowing that despite your teenager's fast-food lunch or the cupcakes at preschool, you're all eating a wholesome meal at dinnertime. And you're the person who made it happen.

The food you lovingly prepare matters because it nourishes and brings your family around the table for a short 20 minutes. It matters because it shapes your children's idea of what "family dinner" is. Does that mean I've never made a box of mac and cheese with a side of applesauce and called it dinner? I've had plenty of those nights. I'm pretty sure these days that it's statistically impossible to make dinner every day (nor do I want to, thankyouverymuch). But most nights, I want our family meal to come from my kitchen, not from a box. If you're reading this, I'm guessing you do, too.

Just because you **LIKE** to cook doesn't necessarily mean you **WANT TO.**

DINNER READY AT SIX? EASY-PEASY!

That's one statement you'll never hear me say! I understand you, too, may be dealing with ringing cell phones or sports practices that have the kids running out the door minutes after they've taken their last bite.

Dinnertime Survival Guide was written to assure you that you're not alone when sometimes making dinner is a pain or your least favorite part of the day. And its goal is to arm you—a parent with your heart in the right place—with a game plan for dealing with the very real obstacles that make it a challenge to pull off.

SOLVING THE NITTY-GRITTY PROBLEMS

This book identifies common obstacles all parents can relate to—like crazy schedules, a tight budget, lackluster skills in the kitchen, or kids who are tugging on your pant leg while you're trying to cook. For every challenge, there are strategies from my own playbook, plus input from experts on how to eliminate it or, at least, how to better deal with it. There's also tried-and-true advice from moms on what actually works. Because when you enlist the help of a bunch of moms on typical dinner dilemmas, you're going to crowdsource some serious wisdom.

The recipes in each section were specifically chosen with each obstacle in mind—so you'll find everything from pork chops that are ready in 15 minutes to a carbonara you can pull together when you swear you have absolutely no food in the house. Your obstacles may change day to day. One evening you're time-crunched, another you're facing bare cupboards. Or they may change as you shift from one stage of parenthood to another. The idea is to flip to the chapter dealing with whatever crisis you're facing *at that moment*. If you head to Chapter 5 while on the brink of a picky-eater impasse, you'll find recipes that appeal to wee folk. If you go to Chapter 10 in a don't-feel-like-it funk, you'll get low-effort, dinner-worthy sandwiches and salads.

GETTING DINNER DONE, NOT PERFECT

I don't expect you to follow these recipes to a T. They've been perfected by the experts in the *Cooking Light* Test Kitchen, who strive to prepare each recipe, and then write it so it's accurate. But let's be honest: Part of what makes you a card-carrying mom is the ability to wing it. Nobody expects you to dash out for pine nuts when all you have is walnuts or make your own breadcrumbs when you have Little League playoffs

HANGRY *adj.*
|ˈhan-ˈgrē|

1. Being so hungry as to become frustrated, angry, and irrational.

2. A state that typically comes over children and spouses roughly 18 minutes before dinner will be ready.

in 30 minutes. So I've included lots of ideas for substitutions, and hereby give you full permission to use what you have and what you like. My kids act like their mouths are going up in flames if I sprinkle red pepper onto anything, so I always leave it out (we parents sprinkle it onto our own portions). Likewise, if an ingredient seems too pricy for your budget, simply sub in something less expensive.

JUST-RIGHT RECIPES FOR FAMILIES

Rest assured, I included recipes for macaroni and cheese, spaghetti, and easy stove-top pork chops. It made total sense to include varieties of meat loaf, lasagna, and tacos. And it was also important to pick a few recipes to broaden kids' horizons—like Roasted Brussels Sprouts and Apples and hot pink Beet and Brown Rice Sliders. No matter what, each recipe had to pass my uncompromising tests:

1. Could I find these ingredients in a grocery store? I don't expect you to spend your savings at gourmet markets or your valuable time hunting for obscure ingredients. Some recipes call for items in the ethnic-foods section of your store—but I also try to give substitutions when possible.

2. Could I make it in a reasonable amount of time? A few of these recipes are ideal for weekends, when you typically have extra hours (and the help of your spouse and maybe kids). Otherwise, most are recipes you can pull together in less than an hour, most in less than 30 minutes.

3. Would my kids eat it? I've flipped through many a family cookbook and thought, "My kids won't eat that. Or that. Or that." My two boys aren't off-the-charts picky, but they're typical kids who prefer the basics and occasionally grouse at flecks of parsley. I spent months making *Cooking Light* recipes and tinkering with the ones from my own recipe book. I loved answering the question of "What are we

BRINNER *n.*

|brin-nər|

1. A dinner that consists of traditional breakfast foods, such as pancakes, eggs, and bacon.

2. A meal with the magical power to erase bad days and cheer even the grouchiest of children.

having for dinner?" with something like "Cider-Glazed Chicken with Browned Butter–Pecan Rice and Easy Garlic-Roasted Kale." Happily, my kids approached it like a fun science experiment, using a rating system of thumbs up, thumbs down, or thumbs sideways. They liked most of what I made. But it's also an unfortunate fact that my older son, Henry, hates brown rice and neither child will eat salmon, so clearly they couldn't be entrusted with the final decision—and a thumbs-down review didn't always mean a recipe was nixed.

WHO AM I?

I'm certainly not a chef. After college, I somehow kept myself fed with pasta and jarred sauce, tuna in foil pouches, and take-out salads. Eventually, I taught myself how to pull together a decent meal. Since getting married and having kids, I've upped my game and invested more effort into making meals really count.

I'm also not a food snob. I grew up on meat and potatoes, and still really love the basics: bubbly macaroni and cheese or a slow-cooked pot roast. Though eating a diet of mostly unprocessed foods is a priority, I don't cook with all organic ingredients or make everything from scratch. Over the years, I've discovered how delicious and surprisingly simple it is to make homemade pizza and salad dressing myself, so you'll find those here. But I'm also not above buying a bottle of ranch dressing or using chicken stock from a carton.

I'm a registered dietitian, so I have one eye on getting the meal done and another on making sure it's balanced. I'm also a big believer in the value of family dinner: With every meal, I'm teaching my kids our food values, the taste of real ingredients, and habits that will carry them into adulthood. I'm also a little bit frazzled. Most days, I'm just trying to keep my head above water in a sea of soccer practices, PTA committees, laundry, lunch packing, and nose wiping.

But most importantly, I'm the mother of two school-aged boys, who bring much joy and noise to my life. And Legos®. They come with an awful lot of Legos.

IT'S A FAMILY AFFAIR
in my household (and this book)

*In my house, I'm the primary cook. That's partly out of necessity because I'm home earlier. It's also possible that I'm a wee bit of a control freak when it comes to the food that's served in our house, so being the cook is okay with me. What also makes this work: My husband takes care of **every bit** of cleanup after dinner—including packing up the leftovers, loading the dishwasher, and wiping down the counters. I understand that some dads are the chefs (and grocery shoppers) in their households. In others, spouses trade nights. So dads, if you are reading this and I refer to "moms" too much in this book, I apologize—it's only because I am one.*

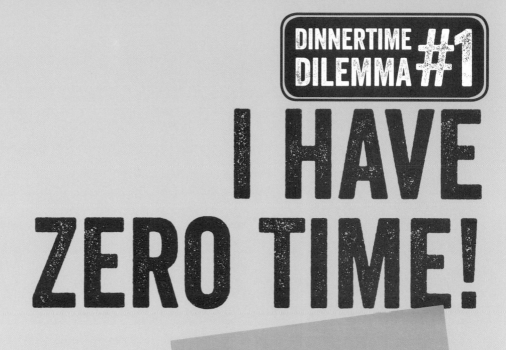

DINNERTIME DILEMMA #1

I HAVE ZERO TIME!

Speedy Recipes
Save the Day

Time. It's a funny thing. A half hour can stretch into eternity when it's been a very long day with my kids and I'm waiting for the minutes to tick down to their bedtime. But at 5:30 p.m., those same 30 minutes can feel like a race against the clock in the kitchen—a fight for every last second before we have to dash out the door for soccer practice or piano lessons.

It doesn't matter if you work outside the house or are home all day with children. Most nights of the week, there never seems to be enough time to make dinner. **But with the strategies and recipes on the following pages, dinner prep can start to feel a lot less frantic.**

TRY THIS!

Batch cook with your new best friend.

It's the gallon-size zip-top bag. In it, you can hold a dinner-ready portion that will save your sanity. It's also the best way to make the most of precious freezer real estate. Just double or triple your favorite dinner recipe, and freeze one portion—or two—for when time is scarce. Fill the bags and remove as much air as possible. Seal and press them flat. Use a permanent marker to label the bags with the name of contents, date, and cooking instructions, and stack them in your freezer. If this project sounds a bit too ambitious, consider the following two ways to make it happen while lightening your load.

Cook with your spouse.

Remember those pre-kid days when you leisurely cooked meals together? Cooking together was fun, and still can be. But now with kids, weekends are usually the ideal time to get a head-start on weeknight meals. Set the little ones with toys or a lengthy movie with bonus features and batch cook together. Then during the week, whichever parent is home first will be familiar with the meal that awaits in the freezer and can get it started before the kids get the notion to storm the snack cabinet or become un-bearably cranky.

Cook with your friends.

A friend of mine and I get together occa-sionally for "freezer cooking nights." We plan out our recipes ahead of time, split up the grocery list, and spend an evening in the kitchen cooking and catching up. Truth be told, we often get so carried away catching up that we forget to add the salt or double the breadcrumbs. But by the end of the evening, we both have at least a week's worth of freezer-ready meals—and feel rejuvenated by our time together.

Start meal planning.

For years I considered meal planning a nice idea in theory—something that more organized moms did after frosting 100 cupcakes for the PTA bake sale and refilling their label makers. But now I consider it an essential task, on par with taking out the trash and washing dirty laundry. Because when I map out meals, my week goes smoothly and dinner falls into place every night (okay, *most nights*). When I wing it, I end up scouring the cupboards at 4:30 in the afternoon, and when I'm really frazzled, I throw in the towel and order pizza.

It may sound like an arduous chore, but meal planning should take less than 10 minutes. Grab your calendar, cookbook, and laptop or tablet for checking online recipes, and sketch out the week's dinners. Build a simple grocery list, and then check to see what ingredients you already have. Of the seven days in a week, the circum-stances in the chart on the following page typically drive the recipes I select.

That leaves one night that's easy on the cook and budget friendly. On "leftover night," we clean out the refrigerator and eat up every last bite.

(Continued)

When it comes down to it, meal planning is really a small time investment considering the dividends: no more what's-for-dinner panic, no more return trips to the store, no more 4:30 p.m. stress.

Though my typical meal-planning system is low-tech (I scribble the week's plan on a pad of paper I keep in a kitchen drawer), there are lots of apps and websites to help. These come recommended by my tech-savvy friends.

For planning meals:
- Plantoeat.com
- Thescramble.com
- Pepperplate.com

For building grocery lists:
- Ourgroceries.com
- Groceryiq.com
- Ziplist.com

SALLY'S WEEKNIGHT PLAN

KIDS' WEEKNIGHT ACTIVITIES	HOW TO GET DINNER ON THE TABLE
PRACTICE OR LESSON NIGHTS (1 TO 2 PER WEEK)	Slow-cooker recipes are my go-to choices for karate, soccer, and swimming kind of evenings.
WEEKNIGHTS AT HOME (2 TO 3 PER WEEK)	On these evenings, homework, play, and kids' chores take up our time. I plan on meals that take about 30 to 45 minutes to get to the table.
DINING-OUT NIGHT (1 PER WEEK)	Or it might be calling the restaurant for take-out. Either way, ignoring this reality would be impractical.
FUN WEEKEND MEAL (1 PER WEEK)	These nights might take a little extra time and might require the help of my husband!

Bust out your slow cooker.

At the risk of sounding dramatic, it will single-handedly save dinnertime. The first night you walk through the door at 5:30 and are greeted by the aroma of a hot meal that you have only vague memories of prepping while you were still in your bathrobe, you'll be hooked.

Though slow cookers are pretty foolproof, most people have suffered a slow-cooker fail at some point. Mine was mushy, tasteless overnight oatmeal. Since Crock-Pot® is the household name for slow cookers, I went straight to them with my most burning questions. Here are their expert answers.

Do I really need to brown or sear meat before putting it in the slow cooker?

Technically, you don't *have* to brown or sear the meat (the exception is ground beef, which will turn into a greasy clump if not browned first), so if you're feeling extra time-crunched, go ahead and skip it. But that extra step of caramelizing the surface does add a richer, deeper flavor to the finished product that's probably worth creating extra dirty dishes. Another perk: You'll be able to melt off some of the meat's fat and pour it off before adding the meat to the slow cooker.

Why is my chicken always dry?

It's a lack of liquid. The rule of thumb is at least 1 to 2 cups of liquid—such as water, broth, or some kind of sauce—for a standard-size slow cooker.

Should I cook on HIGH or LOW?

It really depends on what you are cooking. LOW delivers better results for meats. They'll be more tender, and there's less risk of burning. But the HIGH setting is ideal when you have only a few hours before dinner or if you're cooking a pasta-based dish, like slow-cooker lasagna or macaroni and cheese.

Is it okay to lift the lid during cooking?

Yes, as long as you're not peeking every 10 minutes or leaving the top off for long periods of time. In fact, sometimes there are ingredients you'll want to add near the end of cooking, such as rice, pasta, or dairy products like milk or yogurt. Lifting the lid to stir soups, chilis, and stews a few times while they're cooking is actually a good idea, since it helps prevent burning along the edges.

How long can food really stay on the "warm" function?

A long time—and if you're shopping for a slow cooker, definitely look for this feature. It keeps your meal at a serving-ready temperature for hours. So if you're stuck in traffic or an endless work meeting, you don't need to worry about a cold or scorched dinner.

Cornmeal-Crusted Tilapia with Salsa Verde

Hands-on time: 17 min. Total time: 17 min.

Coating the pan with oil twice helps give these fish fillets a nice crunchy crust. Look for "mild" salsa verde for the sauce if your kids aren't fans of heat—or serve it on the side (a bottle of ketchup for backup is okay, too). This goes great with a side of steamed green beans.

1 cup salsa verde
½ cup cilantro sprigs
¼ cup all-purpose flour
¼ cup yellow cornmeal
1 tablespoon water

1 large egg white
4 (6-ounce) tilapia fillets
¾ teaspoon paprika
2 tablespoons olive oil

1. Place salsa verde and cilantro in a blender; process until smooth.

2. Combine flour and cornmeal in a shallow dish. Combine 1 tablespoon water and egg white in a separate shallow dish, stirring well with a whisk. Sprinkle both sides of fish with paprika.

3. Heat a large nonstick skillet over medium-high heat. Add 1 tablespoon oil to pan; swirl to coat. Dip fish in egg mixture; dredge in flour mixture. Add fish to pan; cook 2½ minutes. Remove fish from pan; add 1 tablespoon oil to pan. Return fish to pan, cooked side up; cook 2½ minutes or until fish flakes easily when tested with a fork or until desired degree of doneness. Serve with salsa.

SERVES 4 (serving size: 1 fillet and about ¼ cup salsa)

CALORIES 316; FAT 10.9g (sat 2g, mono 5.8g, poly 1.4g); PROTEIN 36.5g; CARB 16.4g; FIBER 0.7g; CHOL 85mg; IRON 1.5mg; SODIUM 564mg; CALC 21mg

SLOW-COOKER Lasagna

Hands-on time: 14 min. Total time: 3 hr. 14 min.

I'd written off slow-cooker lasagna after too many mushy results. But this recipe changed my mind. The noodles turn out soft but still slightly chewy. I knew it was a big hit when, after taking his first bite, my son asked, "There's more of this, right?"

1 pound ground sirloin
1 cup sliced fresh mushrooms
1 teaspoon dried Italian seasoning
2 teaspoons bottled minced garlic
⅓ cup water
½ teaspoon salt
1 (24.5-ounce) jar organic pasta sauce (such as Amy's)

6 ounces shredded part-skim mozzarella cheese (about 1½ cups), divided
½ (15-ounce) carton part-skim ricotta cheese
Cooking spray
8 uncooked lasagna noodles
Basil leaves (optional)

1. Cook beef, mushrooms, Italian seasoning, and garlic in a large nonstick skillet over medium-high heat until beef is browned, stirring to crumble. Drain.

2. Combine ⅓ cup water, salt, and pasta sauce in a medium bowl; stir well. Combine 1 cup mozzarella cheese and ricotta cheese in another medium bowl; stir well.

3. Spread ½ cup pasta sauce mixture in bottom of a 4-quart electric slow cooker coated with cooking spray. Arrange 4 noodles in bottom of slow cooker, breaking noodles to fit. Spoon half of beef mixture over noodles; top with half of remaining pasta sauce mixture. Spoon ricotta cheese mixture over sauce. Place remaining 4 noodles over ricotta cheese mixture, breaking to fit. Spoon remaining half of beef mixture over noodles; top with remaining pasta sauce mixture. Sprinkle with ½ cup mozzarella cheese. Cover and cook on HIGH for 3 hours or until sauce is bubbly and noodles are done. Garnish with basil leaves, if desired.

SERVES 8 (serving size: ⅛ of lasagna)

CALORIES 280; **FAT** 10.9g (sat 5g, mono 3.5g, poly 0.5g); **PROTEIN** 21.6g; **CARB** 21.8g; **FIBER** 2.9g; **CHOL** 55mg; **IRON** 2.7mg; **SODIUM** 741mg; **CALC** 231mg

CRAZY TRICK
that actually works!

Even if they're not labeled "no boil" noodles, you can use regular lasagna noodles in the slow cooker or the oven without boiling them first. Just be sure to use a generous amount of pasta sauce in the pan and on top of the noodles. And cover it with the lid while slow cooking or tightly with foil during baking.

Beef Stroganoff

Hands-on time: 25 min. Total time: 25 min.

This dish earned the coveted "double thumbs up" from my kids, who added Parmesan over their helpings and cleaned their plates. Try this time-saving plan: In the morning, slice the flank steak, chop your onions and parsley, and refrigerate until ready to cook.

6½ cups water, divided
4 ounces uncooked egg noodles
1 pound flank steak, trimmed
Cooking spray
1 cup chopped onion
½ teaspoon kosher salt
½ teaspoon black pepper
¼ teaspoon hot paprika
1 (6-ounce) package presliced exotic mushroom blend
1 cup lower-sodium beef broth, divided
5 teaspoons all-purpose flour
⅓ cup fat-free sour cream
3 tablespoons thinly sliced green onions
1 tablespoon butter
2 tablespoons chopped fresh flat-leaf parsley

1. Bring 6 cups water to a boil in a large saucepan. Add noodles; cook 5 minutes or until al dente. Drain.

2. Cut beef across the grain into ¼-inch-wide strips; cut strips into 2-inch pieces.

3. Heat a large skillet over medium-high heat. Coat pan with cooking spray. Add beef to pan; sauté 4 minutes or until browned. Remove beef from pan. Add 1 cup onion, salt, pepper, paprika, and mushrooms to pan; sauté 4 minutes or until tender. Reduce heat to medium.

4. Combine ¼ cup beef broth and flour in a small bowl, stirring with a whisk. Add broth mixture, beef, ¾ cup broth, and ½ cup water to pan, scraping pan to loosen browned bits. Cover and cook 8 minutes or until sauce thickens. Remove from heat; stir in sour cream, green onions, and butter. Serve beef mixture over egg noodles; sprinkle with parsley.

SERVES 4 (serving size: 1 cup beef mixture and 1 cup noodles)

CALORIES 367; **FAT** 11.9g (sat 4g, mono 3g, poly 0.9g); **PROTEIN** 32.2g; **CARB** 32.1g; **FIBER** 2.4g; **CHOL** 118mg; **IRON** 3.4mg; **SODIUM** 483mg; **CALC** 86mg

Grilled Flank Steak with Soy-Mustard Sauce

Hands-on time: 16 min. Total time: 16 min.

In less than the time it takes your kids to watch an episode of Scooby Doo, you'll have steak and pan sauce ready to go. The trick is making sure your grill pan is hot. You should hear sizzling when you put the meat on. That sears the steak, which locks in the juices. Serve it with mashed potatoes and some grilled veggies or a salad.

1 pound flank steak, trimmed
³/₈ teaspoon kosher salt
¼ teaspoon freshly ground
  black pepper
Cooking spray
1 teaspoon canola oil
1½ teaspoons minced fresh
  garlic

2 tablespoons lower-sodium
  soy sauce
1 teaspoon Dijon mustard
¾ teaspoon sugar
2 tablespoons chopped
  fresh cilantro, divided
1½ tablespoons heavy
  whipping cream

1. Heat a grill pan over high heat. Sprinkle steak with salt and pepper. Lightly coat steak with cooking spray. Add steak to pan; grill 5 minutes on each side or until desired degree of doneness. Let stand 3 minutes.

2. Heat a small skillet over medium-high heat. Add oil to pan; swirl to coat. Add garlic; cook 30 seconds or until fragrant. Add soy sauce, mustard, and sugar; cook 1 minute or until bubbly. Remove pan from heat. Stir in 1 tablespoon cilantro and cream. Cut steak diagonally across the grain into thin slices. Sprinkle with 1 tablespoon cilantro. Serve the sauce with steak.

SERVES 4 (serving size: about 3 ounces steak and about 1 tablespoon sauce)

CALORIES 202; **FAT** 9.7g (sat 3.7g, mono 3.6g, poly 0.6g); **PROTEIN** 25g; **CARB** 2.3g; **FIBER** 0.1g; **CHOL** 45mg; **IRON** 2mg; **SODIUM** 541mg; **CALC** 35mg

Letting the steak rest for 3 minutes after cooking makes it juicier!

DINNERTIME SURVIVAL GUIDE TOP 5

DINNER-TABLE RULES

#1

EVERYONE EATS THE SAME MEALS. No short-order-cook requests will be honored. But don't worry, there will be something you like on the table.

#2

KETCHUP IS ALLOWED. You may put ketchup on anything, but if you start to eat spoonfuls of it plain, the bottle will be removed from the table.

#3

BE NICE TO THE COOK. You don't have to eat everything, or even take a bite, but you may not say "yuck" or "gross."

#4

EAT WHILE THE EATING IS GOOD. If you did not consume your meal, then claim to be hungry 38 minutes after dinner is over, you're in luck! We saved your plate and are more than happy to reheat it for you.

#5

JOIN THE CONVERSATION. Current events or details of the day are welcome, but we are also happy to discuss the ramifications of the melting Arctic sea ice as it relates to Santa's ability to deliver gifts.

Tangy Jam Pork Chops

Hands-on time: 15 min. Total time: 15 min.

My kindergartner, Sam, would eat jam out of the jar with a spoon if I let him. So he's tickled when it suddenly appears on his dinner plate. These pork chops are incredibly fast to pull together. Serve them with rice or couscous to soak up the sweet sauce plus a side of steamed broccoli.

2 teaspoons canola oil
4 (4-ounce) boneless center-cut loin pork chops (about ½ inch thick)
½ cup strawberry jam
2 tablespoons spicy brown mustard
2 tablespoons balsamic vinegar
2 tablespoons lower-sodium soy sauce
2 garlic cloves, crushed

1. Heat a large nonstick skillet over medium heat. Add oil to pan; swirl to coat. Add chops; cook 3 minutes on each side or until browned.

2. While chops cook, combine jam, mustard, vinegar, soy sauce, and garlic.

3. Pour jam mixture over chops. Cover, reduce heat, and simmer 3 minutes or until done. Serve chops with sauce.

SERVES 4 (serving size: 1 pork chop and about 3 tablespoons sauce)

CALORIES 285; **FAT** 8.1g (sat 1.9g, mono 3.6g, poly 1.3g); **PROTEIN** 21.8g; **CARB** 28.4g; **FIBER** 0g; **CHOL** 66mg; **IRON** 0.7mg; **SODIUM** 409mg; **CALC** 23mg

REAL MOM, REAL SMART

I make a big batch of rice in my rice cooker, portion it into plastic freezer bags with 1 to 2 cups per bag, then store it in the freezer. When I need rice, I just pull it out, add a few tablespoons of liquid, and reheat in the microwave.

—Corrine Walker Bell, Springfield, OR

Asian Lettuce Wraps

Hands-on time: 18 min. Total time: 18 min.

A meal that doesn't require utensils equals fewer dishes to wash and, for whatever reason, more food gone from my kids' plates. Iceberg gives these wraps juicy crunch, but you can also use Boston or Bibb lettuce or napa (Chinese) cabbage instead.

2 tablespoons lower-sodium soy sauce

2 tablespoons fresh lime juice

2 teaspoons sambal oelek (ground fresh chile paste)

2 teaspoons dark sesame oil

1¼ pounds ground chicken

1 tablespoon refrigerated ginger paste (such as Gourmet Garden)

½ cup thinly sliced green onions

½ cup matchstick-cut carrots

¼ cup chopped fresh cilantro

¼ cup chopped unsalted, dry-roasted peanuts

12 iceberg lettuce leaves

1. Combine first 4 ingredients in a small bowl. Set aside.

2. Cook chicken and ginger paste in a large nonstick skillet over medium-high heat 7 minutes or until chicken is done, stirring to crumble. Stir in onions, carrots, and cilantro; cook 1 minute. Stir in soy sauce mixture. Remove from heat.

3. Spoon about ⅓ cup chicken mixture and 1 teaspoon peanuts into each lettuce leaf.

Leave out the sambal oelek if your kids don't care for spicy foods.

SERVES 4 (serving size: 3 lettuce wraps)

CALORIES 302; **FAT** 18.2g (sat 4.1g, mono 8.3g, poly 4.6g); **PROTEIN** 26.3g; **CARB** 9g; **FIBER** 2.6g; **CHOL** 94mg; **IRON** 1.2mg; **SODIUM** 497mg; **CALC** 47mg

STOVETOP Macaroni and Cheese

Hands-on time: 10 min. Total time: 31 min.

I'd be lying if I said my boys weren't fans of boxed mac-n-cheese. In fact, my older son, Henry, refers to it as "real macaroni and cheese," as if my homemade versions were somehow imposters. But when I made this recipe, both kids gobbled it up. Lots of scratch macaroni and cheese recipes require baking, but not this one. It skips the baking step in favor of finishing the cheesy noodles with a crisp, buttery topping.

1¼ cups uncooked elbow macaroni (about 6 ounces)
1 cup 1% low-fat milk
2 tablespoons all-purpose flour
5 ounces reduced-fat shredded sharp cheddar cheese (about 1¼ cups)
½ teaspoon salt
⅛ teaspoon freshly ground black pepper
1 (1½-ounce) slice white bread
1 tablespoon butter, melted

Use whole-wheat macaroni for some extra fiber.

1. Cook pasta according to package directions, omitting salt and fat. Drain.

2. Combine milk and flour in a medium saucepan, stirring with a whisk. Cook over medium heat 2 minutes or until thick, stirring constantly with a whisk. Add cheese, salt, and pepper, stirring with a whisk until smooth. Add pasta; toss to coat. Let stand 4 minutes.

3. Place bread in a food processor, and pulse 10 times or until crumbs measure 1¼ cups.

4. Heat a large nonstick skillet over medium heat. Add bread-crumbs, and cook 5 minutes or until lightly browned, stirring occasionally. Stir in melted butter; cook 2 minutes, stirring occasionally. Sprinkle breadcrumb mixture over pasta mixture.

SERVES 4 (serving size: ¾ cup)

CALORIES 334; **FAT** 11g (sat 6.5g, mono 2.8g, poly 0.8g); **PROTEIN** 17.7g; **CARB** 40.3g; **FIBER** 1.7g; **CHOL** 30mg; **IRON** 2.1mg; **SODIUM** 661mg; **CALC** 417mg

Ravioli with Pan-Roasted Tomatoes

Hands-on time: 27 min. Total time: 27 min.

I keep a bag of frozen ravioli on hand at all times for emergency purposes. In minutes, I can make pasta à la I-forgot-we-have-soccer-practice. This recipe is a major upgrade: It starts with refrigerated ravioli (whatever kind strikes your fancy), adds a crispy breading, and then finishes with a quick sauté of sweet grape tomatoes. But it still gets you out the door if you forgot about soccer practice, too.

2 tablespoons water
1 large egg, lightly beaten
1 cup panko (Japanese breadcrumbs)
1/4 cup (1 ounce) grated Parmigiano-Reggiano cheese
1 (9-ounce) package fresh ravioli

3 tablespoons olive oil
4 cups grape tomatoes (about 2 pints)
1/2 teaspoon salt
1/4 teaspoon freshly ground black pepper
3 garlic cloves, coarsely chopped
Basil leaves (optional)

1. Combine 2 tablespoons water and egg in a shallow dish, stirring well. Combine panko and cheese in a shallow dish, stirring well with a fork. Dip each ravioli in egg mixture; dredge in panko mixture.

2. Heat a large skillet over medium-high heat. Add 1 1/2 table-spoons oil to pan; swirl to coat. Add half of ravioli to pan in a single layer; sauté 1 minute on each side or until golden. Remove ravioli from pan using a slotted spoon; drain on paper towels. Keep warm. Repeat procedure with 1 1/2 tablespoons oil and ravioli. Wipe pan with paper towels.

3. Add tomatoes, salt, and pepper to pan; sauté 2 minutes, stirring frequently. Add garlic to pan; sauté 30 seconds, stirring constantly. Divide ravioli among 4 plates; top each serving with tomatoes. Garnish with basil, if desired.

SERVES 4 (serving size: 1/4 of ravioli and 1/2 cup tomatoes)

CALORIES 339; **FAT** 19.2g (sat 6.1g, mono 9.9g, poly 1.6g); **PROTEIN** 14.6g; **CARB** 42.4; FIBER 4.1g; **CHOL** 93mg; **IRON** 1.9mg; **SODIUM** 747mg; **CALC** 159mg

Cake Pan Enchiladas

Hands-on time: 25 min. Total time: 1 hr. 10 min.

Dietitian Katie Morford of Mom's Kitchen Handbook calls herself a lazy cook because she loves to build shortcuts into her recipes. I think her techniques are brilliant. In this recipe, instead of filling and rolling each enchilada one by one, you layer everything in a cake pan, bake, and then serve in wedges.

2 teaspoons extra-virgin olive oil

1/2 cup finely chopped red or yellow onion

2 garlic cloves, crushed

1 1/2 cups frozen whole-kernel corn, thawed

3/4 cup chopped fresh tomato

1 (4.5-ounce) can chopped green chiles, drained

2 tablespoons fresh lime juice

1 (15-ounce) can mild red enchilada sauce

Cooking spray

9 (6-inch) corn tortillas

1 (15-ounce) can black beans, rinsed and drained

1 cup shredded cooked chicken breast

6 ounces shredded sharp cheddar cheese (about 1 1/2 cups), divided

1. Preheat oven to 375°.

2. Heat a large nonstick skillet over medium-high heat. Add oil to pan; swirl to coat. Add onion and garlic; sauté 2 minutes. Add corn, tomato, and chiles; sauté 2 minutes. Stir in lime juice; remove from heat.

3. Pour one-third of enchilada sauce into a 9-inch round cake pan coated with cooking spray. Arrange 3 tortillas over sauce, overlapping slightly. Spread half each of corn mixture, beans, and chicken over tortillas; sprinkle with 1/2 cup cheese. Repeat layers once. Top with 3 tortillas, overlapping slightly. Pour remaining one-third of enchilada sauce over tortillas, and top with 1/2 cup cheese. Cover tightly with foil coated with cooking spray.

4. Bake at 375° for 25 minutes. Uncover, and bake 5 minutes or until cheese is bubbly. Cool 5 minutes; cut into wedges.

SERVES 6 (serving size: 1 wedge)

CALORIES 411; **FAT** 15.4g (sat 6.7g, mono 4.8g, poly 1.5g); **PROTEIN** 25.5g; **CARB** 42.6g; **FIBER** 5g; **CHOL** 62mg; **IRON** 1.5mg; **SODIUM** 548mg; **CALC** 241mg

REAL MOM, REAL SMART

I roast two chickens on a Sunday so I have cooked chicken to toss into quick meals all week long. Ditto for roast beef—I cook a larger one than I need; then I have slices of beef to turn into one or two more dinners.

—Brianne DeRosa, blogger, redroundorgreen.com

Fried Rice with Broccoli and Eggs

Hands-on time: 12 min. Total time: 20 min.

This is one of those perfect "kitchen sink" meals—a nice vehicle for using up whatever veggies you happen to have: a few broccoli florets, half of a chopped bell pepper, a handful of frozen peas. Though chilled rice works best, it's not a must.

3 cups small broccoli florets

4 large eggs

2 tablespoons water

1 tablespoon canola oil, divided

1 tablespoon grated peeled fresh ginger

2 garlic cloves, minced

4 cups cooked long-grain rice, chilled

½ cup shredded carrot

¼ cup fat-free, lower-sodium chicken broth

2 tablespoons lower-sodium soy sauce

2 teaspoons dark sesame oil

¼ teaspoon salt

¼ cup thinly sliced green onions

1. Steam broccoli, covered, 2 minutes or until crisp-tender; rinse with cold water. Drain; cool.

2. Combine eggs and 2 tablespoons water. Heat 1 teaspoon canola oil in a large nonstick skillet or wok over medium-high heat. Add egg mixture; stir-fry 30 seconds or until soft-scrambled, stirring constantly. Remove egg mixture from pan.

3. Add 2 teaspoons canola oil to pan. Add ginger and garlic; stir-fry 30 seconds. Add rice; stir-fry 3 minutes. Add broccoli, carrot, and broth; cook 1 minute. Add cooked eggs, soy sauce, sesame oil, and salt; stir-fry 1 minute or until thoroughly heated. Sprinkle with green onions.

SERVES 6 (serving size: 1⅓ cups)

CALORIES 254; **FAT** 7.8g (sat 1.6g, mono 3.4g, poly 2g); **PROTEIN** 9.9g; **CARB** 36.4g; **FIBER** 3.2g; **CHOL** 142mg; **IRON** 2.6mg; **SODIUM** 362mg; **CALC** 69mg

SMART STRATEGY

Freeze it! Next time you're prepping ingredients or making bread dough, make more than you need and freeze the extra.

Freeze these in heavy-duty zip-top plastic bags:
- *Shredded cheese*
- *Chopped onion, celery, and carrots*
- *Cooked rice*
- *Homemade breadcrumbs*
- *Bread and pizza dough*

Freeze these in ice-cube trays; then pop into heavy-duty zip-top plastic bags:
- *Chopped herbs with olive oil or water*
- *Tomato paste*
- *Chicken, vegetable, or beef broth or stock*

- *Chop a few green onions.*
- *Mix together breadcrumbs and Parmesan cheese for a breading.*
- *Whisk together a marinade.*
- *Juice a lemon or lime.*
- *Chop a handful of fresh herbs.*
- *Combine all the spices you need for a recipe in a small bowl.*
- *Grate a block of cheese.*
- *Measure and rinse lentils or dried beans.*
- *Pound chicken breasts or pork chops thin.*
- *Toast nuts on the stovetop.*
- *Set out any shelf-stable ingredients you'll need for supper.*
- *Place any bowls and measuring cups you'll need on the counter.*

Shortcut Chicken Soup

Hands-on time: 40 min. Total time: 40 min.

The beauty of this homemade chicken soup is that it seems like you've spent all day tending a pot on the stove. Actually, after a trip to the store for stock, pre-cooked brown rice, and two rotisserie chickens, you're done with the hardest part before you even get started.

Cooking spray
1 cup sliced carrot
1 cup chopped celery
1/2 cup finely chopped onion
1 teaspoon minced fresh garlic
1/2 teaspoon salt
1/4 teaspoon freshly ground black pepper
2 (26-ounce) cartons unsalted chicken stock
5 1/2 cups shredded cooked rotisserie chicken
1/4 cup fresh lemon juice
1 tablespoon chopped fresh parsley
1 teaspoon thyme leaves
1 (8.8-ounce) package microwaveable precooked brown rice

1. Heat a Dutch oven over medium-high heat; coat with cooking spray. Add carrot, celery, and onion; sauté 5 minutes. Add garlic; sauté 1 minute. Add salt, pepper, and chicken stock; bring to a boil. Reduce heat; simmer 10 minutes.

2. Add chicken and remaining ingredients; cook 10 minutes or until thoroughly heated, stirring occasionally.

SERVES 6 (serving size: 1 1/2 cups)

CALORIES 286; **FAT** 8.8g (sat 2.2g, mono 2.8g, poly 1.7g); **PROTEIN** 33.5g; **CARB** 18.4g; **FIBER** 1.8g; **CHOL** 85mg; **IRON** 1.3mg; **SODIUM** 653mg; **CALC** 53mg

These are perfect for when you've picked up a rotisserie chicken and want a simple homemade side.

Fluffy Buttermilk Drop Biscuits

Hands-on time: 7 min. Total time: 21 min.

Don't panic when you see clumps forming after mixing the warm butter with the cold buttermilk. That's supposed to happen! And it means your biscuits will be nice and light. Serve them warm with a pat of butter, and let the praise roll in.

5.6 ounces all-purpose flour (about 1¼ cups)
3.6 ounces white whole-wheat flour (about ¾ cup)
2 teaspoons baking powder
1 teaspoon sugar
¾ teaspoon salt
½ teaspoon baking soda
¼ cup unsalted butter
1¼ cups very cold fat-free buttermilk
1 tablespoon canola oil

1. Preheat oven to 450°.

2. Weigh or lightly spoon flours into dry measuring cups; level with a knife. Combine flours, baking powder, sugar, salt, and baking soda in a large bowl, stirring with a whisk to combine.

3. Place butter in a microwave-safe bowl. Microwave at HIGH 1 minute or until completely melted. Add cold buttermilk, stirring until butter forms small clumps. Add oil, stirring to combine.

4. Add buttermilk mixture to flour mixture; stir with a rubber spatula just until incorporated (do not overmix) and batter pulls away from sides of bowl (batter will be very moist).

5. Drop batter in mounds of 2 heaping tablespoonfuls onto a baking sheet lined with parchment paper. Bake at 450° for 11 minutes or until golden. Cool 3 minutes; serve warm.

SERVES 12 (serving size: 1 biscuit)

CALORIES 133; **FAT** 5.4g (sat 2.6g, mono 1.8g, poly 0.6g); **PROTEIN** 3.5g; **CARB** 18.3g; **FIBER** 1.3g; **CHOL** 10mg; **IRON** 1mg; **SODIUM** 305mg; **CALC** 82mg

Lasagna Rolls

Hands-on time: 8 min. Total time: 53 min.

After seeing these in an Italian restaurant, I created my own version at home. They look fancier than a messy piece of lasagna, but they're simple to make.

1 (12-ounce) package whole-wheat lasagna noodles (20 noodles)
1 (24.5-ounce) jar pasta sauce, divided
Cooking spray
12 ounces preshredded reduced-fat 6-cheese Italian-blend cheese (about 3 cups)
2 teaspoons dried Italian seasoning

1 (15-ounce) carton part-skim ricotta cheese
1 (10-ounce) package frozen chopped spinach, thawed, drained, and squeezed dry
1 large egg
2 ounces finely shredded Parmesan cheese (about ½ cup)
Parsley leaves (optional)

1. Preheat oven to 375°.

2. Cook lasagna noodles according to package directions, omitting salt and fat.

3. While noodles cook, spoon 1 cup sauce into a 13 x 9–inch glass or ceramic baking dish coated with cooking spray. Combine Italian-blend cheese and next 4 ingredients (through egg) in a bowl; stir well.

4. Drain noodles, and rinse with cold water. Drain. Place noodles on a flat surface; spread 1 rounded tablespoon cheese mixture over each noodle. Roll up noodles, jelly-roll fashion, starting with short side. Place rolls, seam sides down, over sauce in baking dish. Pour remaining pasta sauce over lasagna rolls.

5. Cover and bake at 375° for 40 minutes. Uncover; sprinkle with Parmesan cheese, and bake an additional 5 minutes. Garnish with parsley, if desired.

SERVES 10 (serving size: 2 rolls)

CALORIES 328; **FAT** 11.1g (sat 5.4g, mono 2.7g, poly 0.4g); **PROTEIN** 25.4g; **CARB** 32g; **FIBER** 6.8g; **CHOL** 47mg; **IRON** 2.1mg; **SODIUM** 605mg; **CALC** 481mg

Grilled Peanut Butter Split Sandwiches

Hands-on time: 15 min. Total time: 15 min.

Sure, these sound more like dessert than dinner, but every once in a while I like to throw my kids a curve-ball. Just to remind them that yes, I really am the best mom in the whole world.

8 (1-ounce) slices firm white sandwich bread, divided
4 teaspoons butter, softened
¼ cup creamy peanut butter
8 teaspoons honey
2 teaspoons semisweet chocolate minichips

4 large strawberries, thinly sliced
2 small bananas, cut into slices
¼ cup pineapple jam

1. Spread one side of each white bread slice with ½ teaspoon butter. Place bread slices, buttered sides down, on a large sheet of wax paper. Combine peanut butter and honey; spread over plain side of 4 bread slices. Sprinkle with chocolate chips; top with strawberry slices and banana slices.

2. Spread pineapple jam over plain side of remaining 4 bread slices. Carefully assemble sandwiches with the buttered sides on the outside.

3. Heat a large nonstick skillet over medium-high heat. Add 2 sandwiches; cook 2 minutes on each side or until lightly browned. Repeat procedure with remaining 2 sandwiches.

SERVES 4 (serving size: 1 sandwich)

CALORIES 436; **FAT** 14.5g (sat 4.2g, mono 6g, poly 3.2g); **PROTEIN** 9.4g; **CARB** 72g; **FIBER** 4.6g; **CHOL** 10mg; **IRON** 3mg; **SODIUM** 497mg; **CALC** 100mg

Balsamic–Blue Cheese Asparagus

Hands-on time: 5 min. Total time: 13 min.

This is a dinner guests–worthy side dish that's simple to make and looks pretty on a serving platter. Be sure to sprinkle on the blue cheese right away, so it melts slightly onto the asparagus spears. Your kids don't like blue cheese? Use Parmesan or shredded mozzarella instead.

1 pound fresh asparagus spears
1 tablespoon balsamic vinegar
2 teaspoons olive oil
1 large garlic clove, minced
2 tablespoons crumbled blue cheese
¼ teaspoon salt
¼ teaspoon freshly ground black pepper

1. Preheat oven to 400°.

2. Snap off tough ends of asparagus; arrange asparagus in a single layer in a jelly-roll pan. Combine vinegar, oil, and garlic; drizzle over asparagus. Bake at 400° for 8 to 12 minutes.

3. Place asparagus on a platter; sprinkle with cheese, salt, and pepper.

SERVES 4 (serving size: about 3 ounces)

CALORIES 63; **FAT** 3.6g (sat 1.1g, mono 2g, poly 0.3g); **PROTEIN** 3.5g; **CARB** 5.5g; **FIBER** 2.4g; **CHOL** 3mg; **IRON** 2.5mg; **SODIUM** 210mg; **CALC** 53mg

CRAZY TRICK
that actually works!

Upgrading your basic S & P to coarse sea salt or kosher salt and freshly ground black pepper really does make a difference. They don't cost much more, but will give your dinners a restaurant-like finish.

Grilled Sweet Potato Circles *(pictured left)*

Hands-on time: 12 min. Total time: 12 min.

My family loves the sweet-salty combo of sweet potato fries. I love anything that lets me avoid turning on the oven in the summertime. That's how this recipe was born. We tend to fight over every last slice around our table, so choose the largest sweet potato you can find to avoid losing some through the grates.

1 large peeled sweet potato (1 pound), cut into ¼-inch slices
1 tablespoon olive oil
½ teaspoon paprika
Cooking spray
¼ teaspoon kosher salt

1. Preheat grill to high heat.

2. Combine sweet potato slices, olive oil, and paprika in a bowl; toss gently to coat. Place sweet potatoes on grill rack coated with cooking spray; grill 4 minutes on each side or until tender.

3. Place sweet potatoes on a platter; sprinkle with salt.

SERVES 4 (serving size: ¼ of sweet potato circles)

CALORIES 73; **FAT** 3.7g (sat 0.5g, mono 2.6g, poly 0.4g); **PROTEIN** 1g; **CARB** 9.5g; **FIBER** 1.6g; **CHOL** 0mg; **IRON** 0.4mg; **SODIUM** 137mg; **CALC** 18mg

REAL MOM, REAL SMART

I took a knife skills class at a cooking school, and now I'm more efficient in the kitchen and less intimidated about preparing foods. Once I improved my skills, I was able to chop things more quickly and feel safer while doing it. And I enjoy the prep—I actually find it relaxing instead of stressful

—Alissa Stoltz, blogger, simplywholesomekitchen.com

The Hulk Spinach Smoothie

Hands-on time: 8 min. Total time: 8 min.

Sam, my 5 year old, wasn't so sure about green stuff in his glass. When I referred to them as "Incredible Hulk Smoothies," he took a sip—and was sold. I'm not suggesting you serve only smoothies for dinner. I am suggesting you serve greens in a glass on the side once in a while just to keep your kids on their toes (and very happy, too).

1 cup plain 2% reduced-fat
  Greek yogurt
6 cups fresh baby spinach
1½ cups plain sweetened
  almond milk

1 tablespoon agave nectar
2 medium peeled frozen
  ripe bananas, sliced
2 kiwifruit, peeled and
  chopped

1. Place yogurt in a blender. Add spinach, almond milk, agave nectar, bananas, and kiwifruit to blender; process until smooth.

SERVES 4 (serving size: 1½ cups)

CALORIES 156; **FAT** 2.6g (sat 0.8g, mono 1g, poly 0.4g); **PROTEIN** 7g; **CARB** 29.4g; **FIBER** 4.7g; **CHOL** 4mg; **IRON** 1.6mg; **SODIUM** 134mg; **CALC** 153mg

MAKE-AHEAD Chocolate–Peanut Butter Pudding

Hands-on time: 6 min. Total time: 8 min.

Never mind boxed pudding mix and its long list of ingredients. This one cooks up in just about the same time. My kids both licked their bowls clean. And when I confessed that I'd used one of the leftover chocolate Easter bunnies without their permission, they didn't even care.

1/3 cup granulated sugar
2 tablespoons cornstarch
2 tablespoons Dutch
   process cocoa
1 1/2 cups 1% low-fat milk
1/2 cup half-and-half
2 ounces milk chocolate,
   finely chopped

1/4 cup creamy peanut
   butter
1 tablespoon chopped
   unsalted, dry-roasted
   peanuts
12 banana slices (optional)

1. Combine sugar, cornstarch, and cocoa in a medium saucepan; stir with a whisk. Add milk and half-and-half, stirring with a whisk. Bring to a boil over medium-high heat. Cook 1 minute or until thick and bubbly, stirring constantly.

2. Remove from heat. Add chocolate and peanut butter, stirring until smooth. Spoon pudding into each of 6 bowls. Top each serving with peanuts. Garnish with banana slices, if desired.

You can use natural or regular PB here.

SERVES 6 (serving size: 1/3 cup pudding and 1/2 teaspoon peanuts)

CALORIES 235; **FAT** 12g (sat 4.8g, mono 4.6g, poly 2g); **PROTEIN** 6.9g; **CARB** 26.7g; **FIBER** 1.4g; **CHOL** 13mg; **IRON** 1.1mg; **SODIUM** 98mg; **CALC** 119mg

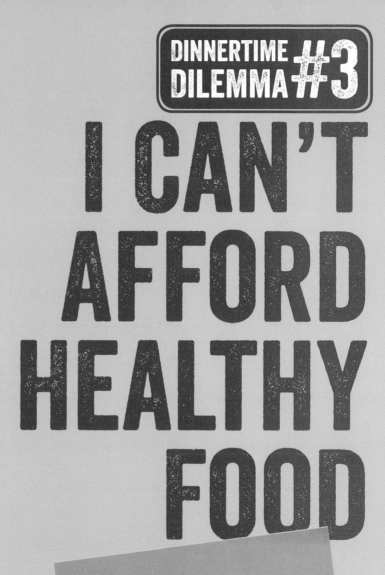

I CAN'T AFFORD HEALTHY FOOD

Save Bucks with Thrifty Dishes

I was a coupon clipper long before reality shows made it seem like some kind of mental health diagnosis. But as much as I love nabbing a good bargain, there are many days when I wish I could simply wheel my cart into the store and load it up without looking at prices, considering sales, or consulting my coupons (or ditch the kitchen completely and eat out every time I didn't feel like cooking). But I can't. I have a mortgage, car payments, and, therefore, a food budget that influences what I buy, what I cook, and how often we head out to a restaurant. I'm guessing you do, too.

Thankfully, a budget doesn't have to stand between you and a home-cooked meal your family will happily scarf down. **Bottom line: You can still be frugal and eat really, really well.**

TRY THIS!

Get smarter at the store.

The grocery store can be a dangerous place for an unsuspecting shopper. There are displays that look like bargains but totally aren't, impulse purchase opportunities at every turn, and complicated promotions that require you to do long division in your head. If you're serious about sticking to a budget, you can't just wander in with your credit card and a fuzzy mental list of what you need. That's like going into battle with a cap gun.

Smart shopping starts at home with meal planning (see page 17). As you're mapping out your meals, dig the store circulars out of the recycling bin and scan the front pages for the week's "loss leaders." That's retail-speak for items priced too low to resist in the hope that you'll also pick up a bunch of other expensive stuff you weren't planning to buy. Build some meals around those sale items. And purchase absolutely everything you need for the week. I can't tell you how many times I have fallen prey to running into the store for just an onion, only to come out with four bags of groceries. Learn from my mistakes, and make a pact with yourself to eliminate return trips to the store. I promise you'll save money if you'll use the following strategies.

1. Keep a cost book. Make a master list of the items you buy regularly, and then track them for a few weeks to figure out their lowest price. You'll instantly know when the price is right, and can stockpile them when prices hit rock bottom.

2. Be brand flexible. Store brands have greatly improved. There may be items you won't budge on, like your favorite brand of cereal. But since store brands typically cost less than name brands, it makes economic sense to use them.

3. Check unit prices. That's the price per unit measurement (like ounces), and it's the best way to compare costs. At most stores, it's listed in fine print on the price tag on the shelf. If it's not there, simply divide the cost by the unit measurement.

4. Watch shrinking package sizes. Take note, shoppers. What looks like a pound of pasta is often less. Downsizing is one way manufacturers are dealing with rising costs, so be sure you're getting the usual amount.

Go meatless.

Meat and poultry tend to take the biggest bite out of an average grocery bill—especially if you're trying to buy organic. You can start by simply using less meat in a dish than called for. Shredded chicken goes further than whole chicken breast halves, and you can combine ground beef with beans for burritos.

Plan at least one to two vegetarian meals every week, and you'll cut costs dramatically. You can easily cook four servings of beans or eggs for less than a buck. I asked Danielle Omar, registered dietitian, vegetarian, and blogger at foodconfidence.com, for some tips on eating meat-free more often. Here's what she had to offer:

(Continued)

1. Go easy on faux meat. Packaged soy burgers, soy dogs, and meatless chicken nuggets are typically highly processed, which is a sign they'll be high in sodium and ingredients like artificial color. If you want to create a meat-like feel to dinners, buy tofu (organic, if possible) or fermented tempeh, a probiotic that offers healthy bacteria.

2. Create filling meals. It's the protein in meals that's satisfying, and there are countless high-protein vegetarian options. Build meals around foods like beans, lentils, eggs, nuts, seeds—like sunflower and pumpkin—and high-protein grains like quinoa.

3. Stick to familiar stuff. A lot of traditional comfort foods like lasagna, enchiladas, and even burgers can easily be made meatless. Lentils are an ideal substitute for ground beef. Chopped, sautéed mushrooms can stand in for meat in lasagna.

Stop wasting food.

Imagine yourself taking a $50 bill from your wallet, stuffing it down your kitchen drain, and then turning on the disposal. Every week. Turns out, the average American family actually pitches 20 pounds of food every month—or as much as $200 thrown away monthly. Stopping that kind of waste is key if you want to stay on budget. One way to start is to simply think twice before tossing food. Sour milk may be a no-brainer, but not everything deserves to be chucked because it's slightly past its prime. Here are some ideas for making your money work hard to the last cent.

BE RESOURCEFUL

Consider these second acts for the stragglers in your kitchen before tossing them out.

Fresh Produce: Slice up fruit, and freeze it for smoothies. Chop leftover veggies like a stray carrot or half an onion, and toss into a freezer bag for future soups and slow-cooker dishes.

Cheese: Moldy sections can simply be cut off. Odds and ends can be thrown into homemade macaroni and cheese.

Yogurt: Has the "Best By" date passed? Yogurt is usually good 1 to 2 weeks after that stamped date. Freeze yogurt you can't use now into cubes for smoothies.

Bread: Toss rejected end pieces into the food processor for quick homemade breadcrumbs.

Crackers & Chips: Crush stale snacks by hand or with a food processor to use as breading on chicken or fish.

Coffee: Pour leftover brewed coffee into ice cube trays to make frozen coffee drinks or to cool down piping hot coffee. Same thing for wine—cubes of frozen wine can be put into soups or used to deglaze a pan.

Herbs: Chop the last of the herbs, and add to ice cube trays that are filled with water or olive oil before freezing.

Tuna Noodle Casserole

Hands-on time: 27 min. Total time: 32 min.

Your mom may have made a version of this, likely with a can of cream-of-something soup. She made it because it was easy, fast, and didn't cost much—and because a hot, bubbly casserole made everyone feel good at the end of a long day. You'll get the same perks from this one, minus the soup can.

8 ounces uncooked wide egg noodles

2 tablespoons olive oil

1/2 cup chopped yellow onion

1/3 cup chopped carrot

2 tablespoons all-purpose flour

2 3/4 cups fat-free milk

4 ounces 1/3-less-fat cream cheese (about 1/2 cup), softened

2 tablespoons Dijon mustard

1/2 teaspoon freshly ground black pepper

1/4 teaspoon salt

1 cup frozen peas, thawed

2 ounces grated Parmigiano-Reggiano cheese (about 1/2 cup), divided

2 (5-ounce) cans solid white tuna in water, drained and flaked

Cooking spray

1. Preheat broiler.

2. Cook noodles according to package directions, omitting salt and fat. Drain. Heat a large skillet over medium heat. Add oil to pan; swirl to coat. Add onion and carrot; cook 6 minutes or until carrot is almost tender, stirring occasionally. Sprinkle with flour; cook 1 minute, stirring constantly. Gradually stir in milk; cook 5 minutes, stirring constantly with a whisk until slightly thick. Stir in cream cheese, mustard, pepper, and salt; cook 2 minutes, stirring constantly.

3. Remove pan from heat. Stir in noodles, peas, 1/4 cup Parmigiano-Reggiano cheese, and tuna. Spoon mixture into a shallow broiler-safe 2-quart glass or ceramic baking dish coated with cooking spray; sprinkle with 1/4 cup Parmigiano-Reggiano cheese. Broil 3 minutes or until golden and bubbly. Let stand 5 minutes before serving.

SERVES 6 (serving size: 1 1/3 cups)

CALORIES 422; FAT 16.5g (sat 7.1g, mono 6.3g, poly 1.8g); PROTEIN 27.4g; CARB 40.6g; FIBER 3g; CHOL 88mg; IRON 2.4mg; SODIUM 608mg; CALC 293mg

STOVETOP Tilapia with Smoked Paprika

Hands-on time: 8 min. Total time: 16 min.

Consider this equation: One of the most affordable types of fish you can buy + spices you probably already have in your cabinet = a fast, simple, and inexpensive weeknight meal. Serve it alongside a bright green veggie like green beans, broccoli, or asparagus and a grain like polenta or couscous.

1 teaspoon smoked paprika
½ teaspoon garlic powder
¼ teaspoon salt
¼ teaspoon freshly ground black pepper

4½ teaspoons olive oil
4 (6-ounce) tilapia fillets
Cooking spray
Flat-leaf parsley leaves (optional)

1. Heat a large nonstick grill pan over medium-high heat.

2. Combine paprika, garlic powder, salt, pepper, and oil in a bowl, stirring well. Rub fish with oil mixture.

3. Coat pan with cooking spray. Add fish to pan; cook 4 minutes on each side or until fish flakes easily when tested with a fork or until desired degree of doneness. Garnish with flat-leaf parsley, if desired.

SERVES 4 (serving size: 1 fillet)

CALORIES 422; **FAT** 9.7g (sat 3g, mono 5.1g, poly 1.1g); **PROTEIN** 39.9g; **CARB** 34.2g; **FIBER** 4.1g; **CHOL** 73mg; **IRON** 1mg; **SODIUM** 751mg; **CALC** 414mg

CRAZY TRICK
that actually works!

Instead of the traditional spice aisle, head to the ethnic foods section of your grocery store. The spices there are typically less expensive than the spices found elsewhere in the supermarket.

Grilled Asian Flank Steak with Mango Salad

Hands-on time: 32 min. Total time: 52 min.

If you consider steak a budget-buster, try flank steak. It's a less-expensive cut that cooks up quickly.

1/4 cup chopped fresh cilantro

5 teaspoons sugar, divided

1 tablespoon grated peeled fresh ginger

1 tablespoon minced fresh garlic

1 tablespoon fish sauce

1 tablespoon lower-sodium soy sauce

1 (1-pound) flank steak, trimmed

Cooking spray

3 tablespoons fresh lime juice

2 tablespoons water

1 tablespoon creamy peanut butter

1/2 teaspoon crushed red pepper

3 cups shredded romaine lettuce

2 cups shredded green cabbage

1/2 cup mint leaves

1/2 cup cilantro leaves

1/4 cup thinly sliced green onions

1 mango, peeled and diced

1. Preheat grill to medium-high heat.

2. Combine chopped cilantro, 1 tablespoon sugar, and next 4 ingredients (through soy sauce) in a large zip-top plastic bag. Add beef; let stand 15 minutes. Remove beef from marinade; reserve marinade.

3. Place beef on grill rack coated with cooking spray. Drizzle with reserved marinade. Grill 5 minutes on each side or until desired degree of doneness. Remove from grill; cover with foil. Let stand 5 minutes; cut beef across the grain into thin slices.

4. Combine lime juice, 2 tablespoons water, peanut butter, 2 teaspoons sugar, and pepper in a large bowl; stir with a whisk. Add lettuce and next 4 ingredients (through green onions); toss to coat. Divide salad among 4 plates; top with mango. Serve with beef.

SERVES 4 (serving size: 3 ounces steak and 1½ cups mango salad)

CALORIES 285; **FAT** 8.4g (sat 2.8g, mono 2.4g, poly 0.4g); **PROTEIN** 28g; **CARB** 26.4g; **FIBER** 3.8g; **CHOL** 70mg; **IRON** 2.9mg; **SODIUM** 489mg; **CALC** 81mg

Mix up the marinade in the morning so it's ready to go at dinnertime.

Pork Tenderloin with Mushroom Sauce

Hands-on time: 21 min. Total time: 51 min.

With a drizzle of the tangy, creamy sauce, this dish looks and feels like a fancy meal—but costs only about $2.50 per serving. Serve with stone-ground yellow grits or polenta.

1 (1-pound) pork tenderloin, trimmed

¾ teaspoon kosher salt, divided

½ teaspoon freshly ground black pepper

2 tablespoons olive oil, divided

1 (8-ounce) package button mushrooms, thinly sliced

3 garlic cloves, minced

2 tablespoons white wine vinegar

1 cup fat-free, lower-sodium chicken broth

¼ cup crème fraîche or sour cream

2 teaspoons Dijon mustard

3 tablespoons chopped fresh flat-leaf parsley (optional)

1. Place a small roasting pan in oven. Preheat oven to 425°.

2. Sprinkle pork with ½ teaspoon salt and pepper. Add 1 tablespoon oil to preheated pan, and swirl to coat. Add pork to pan. Bake at 425° for 20 minutes or until a thermometer registers 145°, turning after 10 minutes. Remove pork from pan, and let stand 10 minutes.

3. Place roasting pan over medium-high heat. Add 1 tablespoon oil to pan; swirl to coat. Add mushrooms; sauté 4 minutes, stirring occasionally. Add garlic, and sauté 1 minute, stirring constantly. Stir in vinegar, and bring to a boil, scraping pan to loosen browned bits. Cook 1 minute or until liquid almost evaporates, stirring occasionally. Stir in ¼ teaspoon salt and broth; bring to a boil. Cook until liquid is reduced to ⅓ cup (about 7 minutes). Remove from heat; stir in crème fraîche and mustard. Cut pork crosswise into slices, and serve with sauce. Garnish with parsley, if desired.

SERVES 4 (serving size: 3 ounces pork and about 2½ tablespoons sauce)

CALORIES 257; **FAT** 15.2g (sat 5.2g, mono 6.1g, poly 1.2g); **PROTEIN** 25.3g; **CARB** 3.7g; **FIBER** 1g; **CHOL** 76mg; **IRON** 1.7mg; **SODIUM** 575mg; **CALC** 20mg

SMART STRATEGY

Take inventory. Make a list of everything you have in your refrigerator, freezer, and pantry. Plan meals using those ingredients, and buy only the extras you'll need. Expect to spend about half of your usual budget. When I do this, my weekly grocery bill ranges from $25 to $50 for my family of four! We save a lot of money, and it forces me to get creative with what I already have.

Chicken with Honey-Beer Sauce

Hands-on time: 25 min. Total time: 25 min.

Depending on your kids, they'll either giggle scandalously over the name of this chicken or need repeated reassurance that it's not illegal for the under-21 set (my stickler-for-rules first born is in the second group, of course). Use a full-flavored domestic beer like Blue Moon Belgian White Belgian-Style Wheat Ale, and serve with couscous to soak up the yummy dark glaze.

2 teaspoons canola oil

4 (6-ounce) skinless, boneless chicken breast halves

¼ teaspoon black pepper

⅛ teaspoon salt

3 tablespoons thinly sliced shallots

½ cup beer

2 tablespoons lower-sodium soy sauce

1 tablespoon whole-grain Dijon mustard

1 tablespoon honey

2 tablespoons flat-leaf parsley leaves

1. Heat a large skillet over medium-high heat. Add oil to pan; swirl to coat.

2. Sprinkle chicken with pepper and salt. Add chicken to pan; cook 6 minutes on each side or until done. Remove chicken from pan; keep warm.

3. Add shallots to pan; cook 1 minute or until translucent.

4. Combine beer and next 3 ingredients (through honey) in a small bowl; stir with a whisk. Add beer mixture to pan; bring to a boil, scraping pan to loosen browned bits. Cook 3 minutes or until liquid is reduced to ½ cup. Serve sauce with chicken. Sprinkle with parsley.

SERVES 4 (serving size: 1 chicken breast half and 2 tablespoons sauce)

CALORIES 245; **FAT** 4.5g (sat 0.7g, mono 2g, poly 1.1g); **PROTEIN** 40g; **CARB** 7.8g; **FIBER** 0.2g; **CHOL** 99mg; **IRON** 1.6mg; **SODIUM** 544mg; **CALC** 27mg

If you don't have shallots, a diced onion and a minced garlic clove make a fine substitute.

REAL MOM, REAL SMART

I learned how to cut up a whole chicken, which is cheaper than buying pieces in a package. One whole chicken can provide three meals for us: One meal of legs and thighs, one meal with breast meat, and a pot of chicken stock with the back and breast bones. I freeze whatever we can't use right away.

—Amy Quinn, Mullica Hill, NJ

DINNERTIME SURVIVAL GUIDE TOP 5

SHOPPING WITH KIDS TIPS

#1

TIME IT RIGHT: Feed everyone, including yourself, before you go. (If you must grab something from the shelves in an emergency, don't forget to pay for it.)

#2

INVOLVE YOUR KIDS: Give younger kids the store circular to peruse, and older kids your list to track. Let them make a couple of choices, such as the fruit for their lunchbox or a flavor of yogurt.

#3

STATE EXPECTATIONS: Before going in, explain: "We're not going to get a free cookie at the bakery, but we'll pick out a new cereal."

#4

BE FIRM: Do not give in to meltdowns over checkout-lane candy, no matter how embarrassing, or you'll be in a world of hurt next week. And the next week. And the next one, too.

#5

HAVE AN ESCAPE PLAN: There's nothing wrong with leaving your cart full of groceries with a store clerk and taking your kids to the car for a time-out. You may need one, too.

Skillet Drumsticks

Hands-on time: 34 min. Total time: 39 min.

A package of drumsticks is a whole lot cheaper than chicken breasts—and what kid doesn't like them? These use ingredients you likely already have, and they make good leftovers.

2 tablespoons water
2 tablespoons honey
2 tablespoons balsamic
  vinegar
1 tablespoon brown sugar
1 tablespoon Dijon mustard
1 tablespoon molasses

1 teaspoon minced garlic
1 teaspoon olive oil
6 chicken drumsticks,
  skinned
½ teaspoon kosher salt
¼ teaspoon freshly ground
  black pepper

1. Combine first 7 ingredients in a small bowl, stirring with a whisk.

2. Heat a large nonstick skillet over medium-high heat. Add oil to pan; swirl to coat. Sprinkle chicken with salt and pepper. Add chicken to pan, browning on all sides. Add honey mixture to pan, turning chicken to coat. Reduce heat to medium-low. Cover and cook 15 minutes or until chicken is done, turning chicken every 5 minutes.

3. Uncover and cook 1 minute or until mixture is thick and a mahogany color, and chicken is well coated. Remove from heat; cool 5 minutes. Serve warm or chilled.

SERVES 6 (serving size: 1 drumstick)

CALORIES 180; **FAT** 7.2g (sat 1.8g, mono 3g, poly 1.6g); **PROTEIN** 16.7g; **CARB** 11.9g; **FIBER** 0.1g; **CHOL** 53mg; **IRON** 1.3mg; **SODIUM** 291mg; **CALC** 24mg

SMART STRATEGY

Stock up during seasonal sales. You'll find bargain-basement deals on ketchup and mustard in early July. Prices on stuffing and canned green beans are slashed around the holidays. Since you can use many of these products all year long, pick up extras to squirrel away.

Curried Carrots and Lentils

Hands-on time: 21 min. Total time: 46 min.

This vegetarian dinner is easy on your budget but filling enough that nobody will miss the meat. It combines protein-rich lentils with kid-friendly carrots, and looks pretty with a dollop of Greek yogurt on top. Serve it with jasmine or basmati rice and a simple romaine salad.

2 tablespoons olive oil
1 onion, halved lengthwise and sliced crosswise
1 garlic clove, minced
1½ teaspoons red curry paste
½ teaspoon Hungarian sweet paprika
Dash of ground red pepper (optional)
1 pound carrots, halved lengthwise and sliced

¾ teaspoon kosher salt, divided
1 cup dried lentils
3½ cups water
¼ teaspoon freshly ground black pepper
5 tablespoons plain 2% reduced-fat Greek yogurt
Dill sprigs (optional)

1. Heat a large nonstick skillet over medium heat. Add oil to pan; swirl to coat. Add onion; cook 9 minutes or until lightly browned, stirring occasionally. Add garlic; cook 1 minute. Stir in curry paste, paprika, and red pepper, if desired; cook 30 seconds. Stir in carrots and ¼ teaspoon salt; cook 1 minute. Remove from heat.

2. Combine lentils and 3½ cups water in a large saucepan; bring to a boil. Cover, reduce heat, and simmer 20 minutes. Uncover; increase heat to medium-high, and stir in onion mixture. Cook 2 minutes or until liquid almost evaporates, stirring occasionally. Stir in ½ teaspoon salt and black pepper. Serve warm or at room temperature with yogurt. Garnish with dill sprigs, if desired.

SERVES 5 (serving size: 1 cup lentil mixture and 1 tablespoon yogurt)

CALORIES 353; **FAT** 12.9g (sat 1.9g, mono 8.2g, poly 1.4g); **PROTEIN** 16g; **CARB** 46.5g; **FIBER** 15.8g; **CHOL** 1mg; **IRON** 5.2mg; **SODIUM** 584mg; **CALC** 95mg

CRAZY TRICK
that actually works!

My kids don't like biting into crunchy or slippery pieces of onion. So before sautéing, I quarter an onion and pulse it in a mini-chopper until it becomes a thick paste. Recipes get the onion flavor without the chunky pieces.

Pasta Primavera with Zucchini, Cherry Tomatoes, and Ricotta

Hands-on time: 11 min. Total time: 20 min.

Centering meals around veggies instead of meat is an easy money saver. The creamy ricotta in this simple weeknight pasta adds a richness your kids will love. Feel free to use whole-wheat penne, if your family likes it.

2 cups uncooked penne
1 tablespoon olive oil
2 medium zucchini, halved lengthwise and sliced
1 teaspoon minced fresh garlic
½ teaspoon salt
¼ teaspoon freshly ground black pepper
¼ teaspoon crushed red pepper
1½ cups cherry tomatoes, halved
1 tablespoon butter
½ cup part-skim ricotta cheese
2 tablespoons thinly sliced basil leaves

1. Cook pasta in boiling water 7 minutes, omitting salt and fat. Drain pasta in a colander over a bowl, reserving ¼ cup cooking liquid.

2. Heat a large nonstick skillet over medium-high heat. Add oil to pan; swirl to coat. Add zucchini; sauté 2 minutes. Add garlic, salt, black pepper, and crushed red pepper; sauté 2 minutes. Stir in reserved ¼ cup cooking liquid, tomatoes, and butter; sauté 1 minute or until butter melts. Add pasta, ricotta cheese, and basil to pan; toss gently to coat.

SERVES 4 (serving size: 2 cups)

CALORIES 337; **FAT** 10g (sat 4.2g, mono 4g, poly 0.7g); **PROTEIN** 13.2g; **CARB** 50.2g; **FIBER** 3.7g; **CHOL** 17mg; **IRON** 2.6mg; **SODIUM** 369mg; **CALC** 123mg

SMART STRATEGY

Yes, organics are better for the planet, but not always for your wallet. So be smart with your organic dollars. My advice: Buy organic for the foods your family eats every day and that tend to be high in pesticides. For the rest of the produce, wash well, since a thorough scrubbing can reduce the pesticide residue. Buy lean meats and low-fat dairy if you're buying conventional, since pesticides and chemicals tend to collect in the animals' fat. Here's a list from the Environmental Working Group of common produce that'll help you choose and purchase wisely for your family.

• *Typically high in pesticides, so splurge and buy organic: Apples, blueberries, celery, cucumbers, grapes, hot peppers, imported nectarines, kale, peaches, potatoes, spinach, strawberries, and sweet bell peppers*

• *Typically low in pesticides, so save money and buy conventional: Asparagus, avocados, cabbage, cantaloupe, corn, eggplant, grapefruit, kiwi, mangoes, mushrooms, onions, papayas, pineapple, sweet peas, and sweet potatoes*

Tomato Alphabet Soup

Hands-on time: 18 min. Total time: 38 min.

The alphabet pasta makes this soup a satisfying meal (bonus points for educational enrichment). Serve with crunchy grilled cheese sandwiches or a hunk of bread.

2 tablespoons butter
1 cup chopped onion
1 cup chopped carrot
1/3 cup chopped celery
1 1/2 cups vegetable broth
1 teaspoon dried basil
1/4 teaspoon black pepper

1 (28-ounce) can diced
   tomatoes, undrained
2 cups cooked alphabet
   pasta (about 1 cup
   uncooked pasta)
1 cup 2% reduced-fat milk

1. Melt butter in a saucepan over medium-high heat. Add onion, carrot, and celery; sauté 4 minutes or until tender. Add broth, basil, pepper, and tomatoes, and bring to a boil. Reduce heat; simmer 15 minutes. Stir in 1/2 cup pasta. Remove from heat; let stand 5 minutes.

2. Place half of tomato mixture in a blender. Remove center piece of blender lid (to allow steam to escape); secure blender lid on blender. Place a clean towel over opening in blender lid (to avoid splatters). Blend until smooth.

3. Return pureed soup to pan; stir in remaining pasta and milk. Cook over medium-high heat 2 minutes or until thoroughly heated, stirring frequently (do not boil).

SERVES 6 (serving size: about 1 cup)

CALORIES 175; **FAT** 5.2g (sat 2.9g, mono 1.3g, poly 0.2g); **PROTEIN** 6.1g; **CARB** 279g; **FIBER** 4g; **CHOL** 13mg; **IRON** 1.3mg; **SODIUM** 492mg; **CALC** 93mg

An immersion blender, if you have one, makes this part super easy.

Falafel with Avocado Spread

Hands-on time: 25 min. Total time: 25 min.

Turn an inexpensive pantry staple—canned beans—into hearty meatless patties by adding cheese and crushed tortilla chips.

Patties:
1 (15-ounce) can pinto beans, rinsed and drained
2 ounces shredded Monterey Jack cheese (about ½ cup)
¼ cup finely crushed baked tortilla chips (about ¾ ounce)
2 tablespoons finely chopped green onions
1 tablespoon chopped fresh cilantro
⅛ teaspoon ground cumin
1 large egg white
1½ teaspoons canola oil

Spread:
¼ cup mashed peeled avocado
2 tablespoons finely chopped tomato
1 tablespoon finely chopped red onion
2 tablespoons fat-free sour cream
1 teaspoon fresh lime juice
⅛ teaspoon salt

Remaining ingredients:
2 (6-inch) pitas, each cut in half crosswise
4 thin red onion slices, separated into rings
Mixed salad greens

Chill the pinto-bean mixture for a few minutes to make it easier to form patties.

1. To prepare patties, place beans in a medium bowl; partially mash with a fork. Add cheese and next 5 ingredients (through egg white); stir until well combined. Shape into 4 (½-inch-thick) oval patties.

2. Heat a large nonstick skillet over medium-high heat. Add oil to pan; swirl to coat. Add patties to pan; cook 3 minutes on each side or until patties are browned and thoroughly heated.

3. To prepare spread, combine avocado and next 5 ingredients, stirring well. Place 1 patty in each pita half. Spread 2 tablespoons avocado spread over patty in each pita half; top with onion and greens.

SERVES 4 (serving size: 1 stuffed pita half)

CALORIES 281; **FAT** 9.5g (sat 3.4g, mono 3.9g, poly 1.5g); **PROTEIN** 12.2g; **CARB** 37.4g; **FIBER** 5.9g; **CHOL** 13mg; **IRON** 2.4mg; **SODIUM** 625mg; **CALC** 188mg

EASY Garlic Fries

Hands-on time: 19 min. Total time: 44 min.

My 9-year-old, Henry, thinks drive-thru French fries are the end-all-be-all—but he raved about this Cooking Light reader favorite recipe when we had it alongside burgers one weekend. Amazing what a little bit of butter, garlic, and cheese can do to a batch of simple baked fries.

1½ pounds baking
   potatoes, peeled and cut
   into ¼-inch-thick strips
2 teaspoons canola oil
½ teaspoon salt
1 tablespoons butter

8 garlic cloves, minced
   (about 5 teaspoons)
2 tablespoons finely
   chopped fresh parsley
2 tablespoons grated fresh
   Parmesan cheese

1. Preheat oven to 450°.

2. Combine potatoes and oil in a large zip-top plastic bag; seal bag, and toss to coat.

3. Arrange potatoes in a single layer on a baking sheet lined with parchment paper. Sprinkle with salt. Bake at 450° for 25 minutes or until potatoes are tender and golden brown, turning after 20 minutes.

4. Heat a large nonstick skillet over low heat. Add butter and garlic to pan; cook 4 minutes, stirring constantly. Add potatoes and parsley to butter mixture; toss to coat. Sprinkle with cheese. Serve immediately.

SERVES 6 (serving size: ¾ cup)

CALORIES 140; **FAT** 4.4g (sat 1.7g, mono 1.5g, poly 0.6g); **PROTEIN** 3.1g; **CARB** 22.7g; **FIBER** 2g; **CHOL** 7mg; **IRON** 0.5mg; **SODIUM** 256mg; **CALC** 52mg

REAL MOM, REAL SMART

I avoid the frozen prepared foods at the grocery store, because they often include things that I can buy and make much cheaper on my own. Pasta, sausage, and peppers for three costs much less than a similar frozen dinner—plus it's lower in salt and has leftovers.

—Cami Johnson, Redwood City, CA

Black Bean Hummus

Hands-on time: 20 min. Total time: 20 min.

I like bringing a plate of hummus to the table when I'm serving a light meal such as fish or soup. But if you chop up extra pita and add a pile of dipping vegetables like carrot sticks and pepper strips, you're free to call it dinner, too. This twist on the usual hummus uses black beans instead of chickpeas. Leave out the jalapeño for kids averse to hot and spicy foods.

Look for tahini in the ethnic foods aisle of your grocery store.

½ cup chopped fresh cilantro, divided
2 tablespoons tahini (roasted sesame seed paste)
2 tablespoons water
2 tablespoons fresh lime juice
1 tablespoon extra-virgin olive oil
¾ teaspoon ground cumin
¼ teaspoon salt
1 (15-ounce) can unsalted black beans, rinsed and drained
1 garlic clove, peeled
½ small jalapeño pepper, seeded
3 (6-inch) pitas

1. Preheat oven to 425°.

2. Place ¼ cup cilantro, tahini, and next 8 ingredients (through jalapeño pepper) in a food processor; process until smooth. Spoon into a bowl; sprinkle with ¼ cup cilantro.

3. Cut each pita into 8 wedges. Arrange on a baking sheet. Bake at 425° for 6 minutes, turning once. Serve with hummus.

SERVES 8 (serving size: about 3½ tablespoons hummus and 3 pita wedges)

CALORIES 127; FAT 4g (sat 0.5g, mono 2g, poly 1.1g); PROTEIN 5.1g; CARB 18.5g; FIBER 2.4g; CHOL 0mg; IRON 1.7mg; SODIUM 138mg; CALC 41mg

Chocolate-Granola Apple Wedges

Hands-on time: 12 min. Total time: 17 min.

Enlist your kids' help to dip and coat these fun apple wedges—but be warned that they may want to skip the last step completely, and eat them right away instead.

2 ounces semisweet chocolate, finely chopped

⅓ cup low-fat granola without raisins

1 large Braeburn apple, cut into 16 wedges

Feel free to use whatever variety of apple you have on hand.

1. Place chocolate in a medium microwave-safe bowl. Microwave at HIGH 1 minute, stirring every 15 seconds, or until chocolate melts.

2. Place granola in a shallow dish. Dip apple wedges, skin sides up, in chocolate; allow excess chocolate to drip back into bowl. Dredge wedges in granola. Place wedges, chocolate sides up, on a large plate. Refrigerate 5 minutes or until set.

SERVES 4 (serving size: 4 apple wedges)

CALORIES 132; **FAT** 4.8g (sat 2.6g, mono 1.4g, poly 0.1g); **PROTEIN** 1.5g; **CARB** 23.9g; **FIBER** 2.6g; **CHOL** 0mg; **IRON** 0.8mg; **SODIUM** 22mg; **CALC** 13mg

WHO ATE MY CHEESE? BREAD? SALAD?

Dinners from a Stocked Pantry

Even with the very best meal planning, my refrigerator can start to look more bachelor than mother of two by the end of the week. Instead of calling for take-out, I rely on staples tucked away in my freezer and pantry to see me through. That's when my hoarding tendencies really pay off.

You see, when something's on sale—oatmeal, whole-wheat pasta, canned chickpeas—I always buy multiples (yes, I'm the crazy lady with 10 jars of salsa in her cart). I keep my stockpile on some shelves in our basement landing, an area that my husband and I jokingly dubbed "the bomb shelter." The name stuck, and we now use it so casually that I'm convinced that at some point, one of our children has earnestly informed his teacher, **"My mom keeps extra peanut butter in our bomb shelter."**

TRY THIS!

Stock smarter.
Having these staples on hand means that you'll have *something* that can be made into a meal.

For the refrigerator and freezer:
- ❏ Bags of frozen vegetables and fruits
- ❏ Block or shredded cheese
- ❏ Bottled minced garlic
- ❏ Butter
- ❏ Eggs
- ❏ Frozen chicken breasts
- ❏ Frozen fish fillets
- ❏ Hot sauce
- ❏ Jelly or jam
- ❏ Lemons
- ❏ Mustard
- ❏ Packaged salad greens
- ❏ Salad dressing

For the pantry:
- ❏ Bottled salsa
- ❏ Brown rice
- ❏ Canned or boxed fat-free, lower-sodium chicken, beef, and vegetable broth
- ❏ Cans or pouches of tuna and salmon
- ❏ Dried or canned beans and lentils
- ❏ Bottled pasta sauce
- ❏ Bottled pesto
- ❏ Lower-sodium soy sauce
- ❏ Natural peanut or other nut butter
- ❏ Olive oil
- ❏ Onions
- ❏ Panko (Japanese breadcrumbs)
- ❏ Potatoes
- ❏ Unsalted canned tomatoes
- ❏ Unsalted canned vegetables
- ❏ Vinegar
- ❏ Whole nuts and seeds
- ❏ Whole-wheat pasta

Keep an inventory.
One of the perils of being a hoarder is that I occasionally forget exactly what I have and replace something I didn't need to. Like the night I dashed out to the convenience store at 10 p.m. for ridiculously overpriced butter, and then discovered, a few days later, three pounds of butter in our chest freezer that I had tucked away and forgotten about.

After that, I started taking stock of my pantry, fridge, and freezer. Having some sort of inventory system accomplishes two things: It saves you money because it prevents you from overbuying, and it saves you time and agony on those nights when you swear there is absolutely nothing in the house to eat—because chances are, there is.

Tech-savvy types can use a list app like Evernote. That way, you can access your inventory anywhere, including the grocery store when you're staring at the olive oil and wondering if you need any. Old-schoolers (like me) can use a pen-and-paper list taped to the fridge or inside the pantry door to record things we put in and take out. A friend of mine keeps a magnetic dry-erase board on her refrigerator to inventory her stash. When it's time to make dinner, she just scans the list to see what she has. When she takes something out, she just wipes it off.

(Continued)

GET CREATIVE.

Your cupboards may look bare, but you probably have all the raw materials you need to make a simple, healthy meal. You just don't know it yet. Here are 10 meals to whip up when it appears there's nothing to eat.

Curry Bowl

Canned chickpeas **+** curry powder **+** cooked rice

Quick Quesadillas

Canned refried beans **+** shredded cheddar cheese **+** tortillas

Slow-Cooker Black Bean Soup

Canned diced tomatoes **+** canned black beans **+** frozen corn **+** cumin

Individual Pita Pizzas

Pita bread **+** tomato sauce **+** cheese **+** herbs

Strata

Eggs **+** bread **+** leftover meat, cheese, and veggies **+** onions **+** rosemary

Easy Pasta

Penne **+** canned white beans **+** canned tomatoes **+** garlic

Nutty Asian Noodles

Whole-wheat noodles **+** peanut butter **+** soy sauce **+** frozen carrots

Loaded Potatoes

Sweet potatoes **+** canned black beans **+** salsa **+** shredded cheddar cheese

Salad Niçoise

Mixed greens **+** green beans **+** canned tuna **+** hard-cooked eggs

Simple Fried Rice

Brown rice **+** eggs **+** soy sauce **+** frozen peas

Chip-Crusted Fish Fillets

Hands-on time: 8 min. Total time: 18 min.

The quickest way to get Henry to eat his dinner is to tell him there are potato chips in it—and that he can dip it into ranch dressing. Chips give this fish a nice crunch. The strong vinegar flavor actually mellows during baking.

4 (6-ounce) cod fillets or other firm white fish

2 teaspoons canola mayonnaise

⅛ teaspoon salt

1 (2-ounce) package salt and vinegar kettle-style potato chips, crushed

½ cup light ranch dressing

1. Preheat oven to 400°.

2. Arrange fillets on a parchment paper–lined baking sheet. Brush ½ teaspoon mayonnaise over top of each fillet; sprinkle with salt. Gently press about 2 tablespoons crushed chips on top of each fillet. Bake fish at 400° for 10 minutes or until fish flakes easily when tested with a fork. Serve with ranch dressing.

SERVES 4 (serving size: 1 fish fillet and 2 tablespoons ranch dressing)

CALORIES 291; **FAT** 11.3g (sat 1.2g, mono 5.7g, poly 2.8g); **PROTEIN** 31.7g; **CARB** 14.5g; **FIBER** 0.8g; **CHOL** 79mg; **IRON** 1.4mg; **SODIUM** 549mg; **CALC** 49mg

Plain, barbecue, and sour cream and onion potato chips work great in place of salt and vinegar chips.

Spring Vegetable Carbonara

Hands-on time: 25 min. Total time: 37 min.

I call carbonara "eggs and bacon pasta" because my kids think it's silly. This lightened-up version adds vegetables for some great color. If your kids aren't fans of asparagus or peas, use the veggies they like best.

½ cup frozen green peas, thawed

12 ounces asparagus, trimmed and cut into 1-inch pieces

8 ounces uncooked cavatappi pasta

2 ounces grated fresh pecorino Romano cheese (about ½ cup)

½ teaspoon kosher salt

½ teaspoon freshly ground black pepper

3 large eggs, lightly beaten

4 center-cut bacon slices, chopped

1 cup chopped seeded red bell pepper

1. Cook peas and asparagus in boiling water 3 minutes or until asparagus is crisp-tender; drain. Plunge into ice water; drain. Cook pasta according to package directions, omitting salt and fat. Drain pasta in a colander over a bowl, reserving ¼ cup cooking liquid. Combine pasta and vegetables.

2. Combine cheese and next 3 ingredients (through eggs) in a bowl, stirring well with a whisk. Gradually add cooking liquid to egg mixture, stirring constantly with a whisk. Cook bacon in a large skillet over medium heat until crisp, stirring occasionally. Remove bacon from pan, reserving 1 tablespoon drippings in pan. Add bacon to pasta mixture. Add bell pepper to drippings in pan; cook 3 minutes, stirring occasionally. Add pasta mixture; cook 1 minute or until thoroughly heated, stirring frequently. Remove pan from heat, and stir in egg mixture. Return pan to low heat; cook 2 minutes or until sauce thickens slightly, stirring constantly.

SERVES 4 (serving size: 1¾ cups)

CALORIES 425; **FAT** 14g (sat 5.9g, mono 5.3g, poly 1.6g); **PROTEIN** 22.2g; **CARB** 52g; **FIBER** 5.4g; **CHOL** 183mg; **IRON** 3.6mg; **SODIUM** 614mg; **CALC** 210mg

SMART STRATEGY

A farm share—also known as community supported agriculture or CSA—is like a weekly fresh food subscription. For a monthly or seasonal fee, you get a bag or box every week filled with the farm's harvest, including produce—and sometimes flowers, milk, meat, or even home-baked bread. The benefits of a CSA are huge. You get food that's at the peak of freshness, you support a local farmer, and you're forced (in a good way, of course) to use up your stash each week. To find out if farm shares are available in your community, visit www.localharvest.org.

Whole-Wheat Pasta with Edamame, Greens, and Herbs

Hands-on time: 24 min. Total time: 24 min.

Edamame are young, green soybeans you can buy shelled or unshelled. They're an ideal freezer staple because they take just seconds to cook. They're also high in protein, so they make meatless dishes more filling.

8 ounces uncooked whole-wheat penne (tube-shaped pasta)
1/3 cup fresh lemon juice
3 tablespoons olive oil, divided
1/4 cup chopped fresh flat-leaf parsley
3 tablespoons chopped basil
1 tablespoon chopped fresh thyme
1 teaspoon kosher salt
1 (12-ounce) bag frozen shelled edamame (green soybeans), thawed
3/4 cup fresh corn kernels
1 cup baby arugula
1 cup baby spinach
1 1/2 cups grape tomatoes, halved
6 tablespoons grated fresh Parmesan cheese

1. Cook pasta according to package directions, omitting salt and fat.

2. While pasta cooks, combine lemon juice, 2 tablespoons oil, and next 4 ingredients (through salt) in a large bowl; stir with a whisk until blended.

3. Heat a medium skillet over medium heat. Add 1 tablespoon oil to pan; swirl to coat. Add edamame and corn to pan; cook 4 minutes or until thoroughly heated, stirring occasionally.

4. Drain pasta. Add pasta and edamame mixture to dressing in bowl; toss to coat. Add arugula, spinach, and tomatoes; toss gently. Sprinkle with cheese.

SERVES 6 (serving size: 1 1/2 cups pasta mixture and 1 tablespoon cheese)

CALORIES 325; FAT 12.5g (sat 2.5g, mono 5.9g, poly 2.5g); PROTEIN 14.9g; CARB 39.7g; FIBER 7.3g; CHOL 6mg; IRON 3.5mg; SODIUM 389mg; CALC 136mg

REAL MOM, REAL SMART

I keep cooked rice or pasta in my refrigerator so I can quickly build meals on busy weeknights. I'll mix black beans and cheese with the rice for tacos and burritos, and add a sauce and sometimes meat or cheese to the pasta. A fruit or vegetable on the side, and dinner is done.

—Cassandra Freeland, Columbus, OH

Olive Oil and Garlic Spaghetti

Hands-on time: 13 min. Total time: 26 min.

I don't know about your family, but nobody under my roof complains about a big bowl of steaming, flavorful noodles for dinner. Grown-ups can sprinkle on red pepper for kick, kids can top theirs with Parmesan, and everyone is happy and satisfied.

2 tablespoons extra-virgin olive oil
1/4 teaspoon dried oregano
4 large garlic cloves, minced
4 quarts water
8 ounces uncooked spaghetti
1/2 cup fat-free, lower-sodium chicken broth
2 tablespoons minced fresh parsley

1. Combine olive oil, oregano, and minced garlic in a small microwave-safe bowl. Cover with wax paper, and microwave at HIGH 1 minute.

2. Bring 4 quarts water to a boil in a large stockpot. Add spaghetti; return to a boil. Cook, uncovered, 10 minutes or until al dente, stirring occasionally. Drain. Return to pot. Stir in garlic mixture and broth. Cook over medium heat 4 minutes or until broth is absorbed, stirring constantly. Stir in parsley.

SERVES 4 (serving size: 1 cup)

CALORIES 278; **FAT** 7.7g (sat 1mg, mono 5.1g, poly 1g); **PROTEIN** 7.9g; **CARB** 43.7g; **FIBER** 1.5g; **CHOL** 0mg; **IRON** 2.4mg; **SODIUM** 66mg; **CALC** 20mg

MAKE-AHEAD Chicken-Vegetable Soup

Hands-on time: 13 min. Total time: 20 min.

You can make this quick soup with leftover chicken and whatever veggies your family prefers. There might just be enough leftovers to pour into a lunch-box thermos the next day.

1½ tablespoons extra-virgin olive oil
1 cup chopped onion
½ cup chopped carrot
1 tablespoon minced fresh garlic
½ teaspoon freshly ground black pepper
¼ teaspoon salt
1 thyme sprig
3 cups fat-free, lower-sodium chicken broth
1 (14.5-ounce) can unsalted fire-roasted diced tomatoes, undrained

½ cup uncooked orzo (rice-shaped pasta) or pastina (tiny star-shaped pasta)
5 ounces green beans, cut into 1-inch pieces (about 1 cup)
1 cup shredded skinless, boneless rotisserie chicken breast
2 ounces shaved fresh Parmesan cheese (about ½ cup)

1. Heat a Dutch oven over medium-high heat. Add oil to pan; swirl to coat. Add onion and next 5 ingredients (through thyme) to pan; sauté 4 minutes. Add broth and tomatoes; bring to a boil. Add pasta and beans; cook 5 minutes. Discard thyme sprig. Stir in chicken, and sprinkle with cheese.

SERVES 6 (serving size: 1 cup soup and 4 teaspoons cheese)

CALORIES 257; **FAT** 7.3g (sat 2.5g, mono 3.5g, poly 0.6g); **PROTEIN** 15.4g; **CARB** 32.8g; **FIBER** 3g; **CHOL** 25mg; **IRON** 2mg; **SODIUM** 552mg; **CALC** 145mg

SMART STRATEGY

Use what you have. If you've ever ruled out making a recipe because you didn't have what seemed like a key ingredient, you'll want to dog-ear this page.

Don't have: Breadcrumbs
Use: Cracker, cereal, or chip crumbs or oats ground in a food processor

Don't have: 1 cup of heavy cream or half-and-half
Use: 1 cup whole milk mixed with 1 tablespoon melted butter

Don't have: An egg
Use: 1 tablespoon flaxseed meal whisked together with 3 tablespoons water

EASY Chicken Bagel Pizzas

Hands-on time: 10 min. Total time: 14 min.

Rotisserie chicken gives the humble pizza bagel a satisfying upgrade, and leftover grilled chicken works great, too. Don't skip the step of broiling the bagels before topping them—it keeps them crunchy.

2 (2¼-ounce) plain bagels, sliced in half
½ cup lower-sodium marinara sauce
1 cup shredded skinless, boneless rotisserie chicken breast

4 ounces preshredded part-skim mozzarella cheese (about 1 cup)

1. Preheat broiler.

2. Place bagel halves, cut sides up, on a baking sheet. Broil 2 minutes or until lightly toasted.

3. Spread 2 tablespoons marinara sauce on cut side of each bagel half. Top each half with ¼ cup chicken, and sprinkle with about ¼ cup cheese. Broil 2 minutes or until cheese melts.

SERVES 4 (serving size: 1 bagel pizza)

CALORIES 268; **FAT** 8g (sat 4.2g, mono 2.4g, poly 0.6g); **PROTEIN** 22.1g; **CARB** 32.7g; **FIBER** 1g; **CHOL** 47mg; **IRON** 2.9mg; **SODIUM** 516mg; **CALC** 251mg

SMART STRATEGY

Beware of the food warehouse. Buying food in bulk seems like a good idea on paper—fewer return trips to the store and lower prices, right? But it's not for everyone. If you're hunting for bargains, you may get better deals by combining store sales and coupons at regular grocery stores. Studies also show people tend to serve themselves more from plus-sized packages. And at least at the grocery store you can't impulse buy a cashmere sweater or a flat screen television on your way to the checkout.

DINNERTIME SURVIVAL GUIDE TOP 5 | CONVENIENCE FOODS

#1
BOXED MAC & CHEESE: I choose a version with whole-wheat pasta and no synthetic dyes, and serve it with some fruit or veggies on the side.

#2
PREWASHED BAGGED SALAD GREENS: We eat salad nearly every night, and that wouldn't happen if the greens weren't already chopped and washed by someone else.

#3
WHOLE-WHEAT TORTILLAS: Spread with PB & J, layered with turkey, or stuffed with eggs or leftover ground meat, these regularly come to my rescue at dinnertime.

#4
INSTANT BROWN RICE: Until I master the elusive art of stovetop rice cooking (or admit defeat and buy a rice cooker), I rely on the boxed kind.

#5
CANNED BEANS: After a drain and a quick rinse, they're ready to be whirled into hummus or mashed and added to burritos.

Fancy-Schmancy Ham and Cheese

Hands-on time: 30 min. Total time: 30 min.

You are not a frazzled mom feeding your family ham sandwiches for dinner. You are serving Dijon Croque Monsieurs, which are chichi and international. There's a big difference.

1 tablespoon whole-grain Dijon mustard

1 tablespoon fat-free mayonnaise

8 (1-ounce) slices Italian bread

6 ounces thinly sliced ham

4 ounces shredded Gruyère cheese (about 1 cup)

1/4 teaspoon freshly ground black pepper

1/2 cup egg substitute

1/4 cup fat-free milk

Cooking spray

Use Swiss cheese in place of Gruyère, if that's what you prefer.

1. Combine mustard and mayonnaise in a small bowl. Spread 3/4 teaspoon mustard mixture over each of 4 bread slices; layer each slice with 1 1/2 ounces ham and 1/4 cup cheese. Sprinkle with pepper. Spread 3/4 teaspoon mayonnaise mixture over each remaining bread slice; place bread, mustard sides down, on top of sandwiches.

2. Combine egg substitute and milk in a shallow dish, stirring with a whisk. Dip both sides of each sandwich in egg mixture.

3. Heat a griddle or large skillet over medium heat. Coat pan with cooking spray. Add sandwiches to pan; cook 3 minutes on each side or until lightly browned and cheese melts.

SERVES 4 (serving size: 1 sandwich)

CALORIES 350; **FAT** 11.7g (sat 6.1g, mono 3.1g, poly 0.9g); **PROTEIN** 25.1g; **CARB** 34.6g; **FIBER** 1.7g; **CHOL** 51mg; **IRON** 2.8mg; **SODIUM** 935mg; **CALC** 344mg

CRAZY TRICK
that actually works!

Make scrounging out of the refrigerator feel like a special family tradition. A friend of mine fondly remembers having "Fruit, Bread, and Cheese Night" when the pickings were slim. Her mom put out a platter of fresh fruit, cheese, and bread, and called it dinner. The kids thought it was fun, and it gave her mom a break, too.

Oatmeal Pancakes

Hands-on time: 24 min. Total time: 24 min.

When I declare, "Breakfast for dinner!" I'm instantly supermom in my kids' eyes. For balance, I like to serve pancakes with a side of eggs or chicken sausage and some fruit. Don't have the quick oats that the recipe calls for? Old-fashioned oats will work fine. But do expect the pancakes to have a heartier, chewy texture.

1.1 ounces all-purpose flour
 (about ¼ cup)
1 cup quick-cooking oats
1 tablespoon sugar
½ teaspoon baking powder
½ teaspoon baking soda
¼ teaspoon ground
 cinnamon

⅛ teaspoon salt
1 cup nonfat buttermilk
2 tablespoons butter,
 melted
1 large egg
Cooking spray

If you don't have buttermilk, here's a substitution: Stir 1 tablespoon lemon juice or vinegar into 1 cup milk, and let it sit for five minutes.

1. Weigh or lightly spoon flour into a dry measuring cup; level with a knife. Combine flour and next 6 ingredients (through salt) in a medium bowl.

2. Combine buttermilk, butter, and egg in a small bowl, stirring with a whisk. Add to flour mixture, stirring just until moist.

3. Heat a griddle or large skillet over medium heat. Coat pan with cooking spray. Spoon about 2 heaping tablespoons batter per pancake onto griddle. Cook until tops are covered with bubbles and edges look cooked. Carefully turn pancakes over; cook until bottoms are lightly browned.

SERVES 3 (serving size: 4 pancakes)

CALORIES 273; **FAT** 11.2g (sat 5.7g, mono 3.3g, poly 1.3g); **PROTEIN** 10g; **CARB** 34.7g; **FIBER** 2.8g; **CHOL** 91mg; **IRON** 2.1mg; **SODIUM** 526mg; **CALC** 184mg

Baked Mozzarella Bites

Hands-on time: 15 min. Total time: 18 min.

My fourth grader deemed these "awesome" and just like the ones at a local restaurant that deep-fries everything. In other words, they received his highest praise.

$^1/_3$ cup panko (Japanese breadcrumbs)

3 (1-ounce) sticks part-skim mozzarella string cheese

3 tablespoons egg substitute

Cooking spray

$^1/_4$ cup lower-sodium marinara sauce

1. Preheat oven to 425°.

2. Heat a medium skillet over medium heat. Add panko to pan, and cook 2 minutes or until toasted, stirring frequently. Remove from heat, and place panko in a shallow dish.

3. Cut mozzarella string cheese into 1-inch pieces. Working with 1 piece at a time, dip cheese in egg substitute; dredge in panko. Place cheese on a baking sheet coated with cooking spray. Bake at 425° for 3 minutes or until cheese is softened and thoroughly heated.

4. Pour marinara sauce into a microwave-safe bowl. Microwave at HIGH 1 minute or until thoroughly heated, stirring after 30 seconds. Serve with mozzarella pieces.

SERVES 4 (serving size: 3 mozzarella bites and 1 tablespoon sauce)

CALORIES 91; FAT 10.9g (sat 2.8g, mono 0.3g, poly 0.3g); PROTEIN 7.2g; CARB 6.7g; FIBER 0.1g; CHOL 12mg; IRON 0.3mg; SODIUM 162mg; CALC 162mg

Broccoli with Cheddar Sauce

Hands-on time: 5 min. Total time: 16 min.

If your kids aren't broccoli converts yet, serving it with a nice gooey cheese sauce may be just what you need to win them over.

1 tablespoon all-purpose flour
1 cup fat-free milk
2 ounces reduced-fat shredded extra-sharp cheddar cheese (about 1/2 cup)
3 tablespoons grated fresh Parmesan cheese
1/2 teaspoon Dijon mustard
1/4 teaspoon chopped fresh thyme
1/4 teaspoon salt
1/4 teaspoon freshly ground black pepper
1 1/2 pounds broccoli florets (about 9 cups)

1. Place flour in a medium saucepan. Gradually add milk, stirring constantly with a whisk until smooth. Cook over medium-high heat 3 minutes or until mixture is bubbly and thick, stirring constantly. Remove from heat. Add cheeses, mustard, thyme, salt, and pepper, stirring with a whisk until smooth. Keep warm.

2. Add water to a large saucepan to a depth of 1 inch; set a large vegetable steamer in pan. Bring water to a boil over medium-high heat. Add broccoli to steamer. Cover and steam broccoli 4 minutes or until crisp-tender. Serve broccoli immediately with sauce.

SERVES 8 (serving size: about 1 cup broccoli and 2 tablespoons sauce)

CALORIES 69; FAT 2.3g (sat 1.4g, mono 0.6g, poly 0.2g); PROTEIN 6.2g; CARB 7.1g; FIBER 2.5g; CHOL 7mg; IRON 0.8mg; SODIUM 204mg; CALC 143mg

You can also steam broccoli in the microwave.

Sautéed Apples

Hands-on time: 17 min. Total time: 17 min.

Who says fruit can't pinch-hit for veggies at dinner-time? These sweet, buttery apples make a nice side dish with pork chops, roast chicken, or breakfast for dinner.

3 tablespoons butter
6 cups sliced peeled Granny Smith apples (about 2 pounds)

½ cup packed brown sugar
⅛ teaspoon ground cinnamon

1. Melt butter in a large skillet over medium-high heat. Add apples; sauté 6 minutes or until apples are just tender. Stir in sugar and cinnamon. Cook 1 minute or until sugar melts.

SERVES 4 (serving size: about ½ cup)

CALORIES 137, **FAT** 4.6g (sat 2.7g, mono 1.3g, poly 0.2g); **PROTEIN** 0.2g; **CARB** 25.7g; **FIBER** 1.6g; **CHOL** 12mg; **IRON** 0.3mg; **SODIUM** 49mg; **CALC** 17mg

CRAZY TRICK
that actually works!

If you're forever out of fresh fruits and veggies because they go bad too soon, place a paper towel on the bottom of your produce drawers. It will soak up the moisture that can make fruits and vegetables deteriorate faster.

Chocolate–Peanut Butter Cookies

Hands-on time: 11 min. Total time: 20 min.

These are the perfect cookies to make when you've signed up to bring goodies to the bake sale but don't remember until 9 p.m. the night before. They use just six pantry staples and mix up in one bowl. Natural peanut butter and oats give them a hearty texture.

½ cup old-fashioned rolled oats
¼ cup sugar
¾ cup natural-style creamy peanut butter (such as Smucker's)
¼ cup chocolate-hazelnut spread
1 tablespoon canola oil
1 large egg
½ teaspoon sugar

1. Preheat oven to 350°.

2. Combine first 6 ingredients in a medium bowl; stir until well blended. Drop dough by rounded teaspoonfuls 1 inch apart onto ungreased baking sheets. Make a crisscross pattern on top of each cookie using a fork dipped in sugar.

Dip the fork in sugar to prevent the dough from sticking to the tines.

3. Bake at 350° for 8 minutes or just until tops are no longer glossy. Cool 1 minute on pans. Remove cookies from pans; cool completely on wire racks.

SERVES 38 (serving size: 1 cookie)

CALORIES 56; **FAT** 3.7g (sat 1g, mono 0.3g, poly 0.2g); **PROTEIN** 1.5g; **CARB** 4.4g; **FIBER** 0.5g; **CHOL** 5mg; **IRON** 0.2mg; **SODIUM** 22mg; **CALC** 3mg

I'M NOT A SHORT-ORDER COOK!

Feeding
Picky Eaters

I'm deeply familiar with this problem because I actually was a picky eater as a child—and I drove my poor mother crazy. How crazy? Once, after I requested (but then refused) so many different foods at dinner, my normally sweet and mild-mannered mom poured a glass of chocolate milk over my head. Trust me, I totally deserved it. Thankfully, my kids are much more adventurous than I was—I largely existed on buttered noodles and Steak-umms® for the first 15 years of my life.

But my kids can still be—how do I put this nicely?—challenging at the dinner table from time to time. So believe me, **I understand the impulse to throw in the towel, nuke some chicken nuggets, and call it a day. Resist.**

TRY THIS!

Give your kids a break.

So what if your friend's kids happily devour lobster, leek, and kale cassoulet? Yours don't—at least they don't yet.

Meet your children where they are and be patient. After all, you have decades of experience with food and eating—your kids have just a handful of years. You've probably heard that research shows it can take up to 10 exposures to a food before a child will even try it. But the harsh reality is that it may be more. It could be years. And that's okay. Realize that new food can be intimidating. Kids may not like how it looks, feels, or smells, so they're certainly not going to put it in their mouths. At least, not right away.

Keep in mind that children's appetites also fluctuate widely, sometimes even from day to day. And so do their preferences. Your son or daughter may happily wolf down your meat loaf one night, but grumble the next time you serve it. It's important to respect kids' appetites even though research shows that the majority of parents say they push their kids to eat more.

But if it seems like your kids are refusing their dinner just to mess with you—well, you actually might be right. Children don't have control over too many things in their little lives, so food is one area where they could try to display power and create a huge rise out of their parents. If you don't want to play this game—and believe me, you don't—it's imperative to keep your cool.

Give yourself a break.

Yes, dinnertime can be hard when you're a parent. Sometimes I consider it *bang-your-head-on-the-table, losing-your-marbles* hard. You've just spent 45 frantic minutes pulling together a beautiful meal that contains all the food groups, and your child pushes it away and asks for...string cheese.

Save your sanity and don't escalate the situation into dinnertime drama. Your job as a parent actually ends when you place the healthy meal on the table. You've done your part. Now sit back and eat. No bribing, no cajoling, no spoons-as-airplanes or hostage-crisis-level negotiating. Many dietitians (including myself) follow what's called the Division of Responsibility at mealtime. According to this theory, created by dietitian and feeding therapist Ellyn Satter:

- **The parent decides the what, where, and when of feeding.**

- **The child decides the how much and whether.**

The key is to trust your child to eat as much as she needs. If your kids are used to dinnertime power struggles and being told how many bites to eat, it may take everyone a while to get the hang of this. But in the long run, it's worth it. You'll raise children who know how to listen to their hunger and fullness signals, eat only when they are hungry, and eat only as much as they need.

(Continued)

Make everyone happy.

Keep in mind that most people have at least a few foods they just don't like. So imagine if your spouse cooked dinner for you every night but served your most-hated foods. And when you protested, he said, "Too bad, that's all there is" or, even worse, "No leaving the table until you've cleaned your plate."

A lot of children are serial food flip-floppers: One day they devour eggs, and the next day they consider them super gross. But there are also foods you know your child doesn't like and foods you know he'll reliably eat.

My younger son inhales fruit. My older son never met a chicken breast or pot roast he didn't like. Be sure your dinner table features at least one food you know your kids like, whether it's a favorite side dish or a bowl of carrot sticks. That makes the dinner table a more welcoming,

accepting place. And placing new foods next to old favorites makes those unfamiliar foods seem just a little less scary.

You can also keep your little (and big) people happy by calling a family meeting and asking your kids what they like and don't like about dinnertime. Flip through some cookbooks together for ideas. If they're old enough to choose foods beyond little fish crackers and squeeze yogurts, allow them to select the meal once a week.

And remember: Though picky eating is a normal developmental phase, there are red flags that it could indicate something more. If your child eats fewer than 10 to 20 foods, acts scared or anxious at mealtime, is losing weight, or chokes or coughs while eating, talk to your child's pediatrician. The doctor will likely refer you to a feeding therapist for help.

Bite-Sized Fish Food

Hands-on time: 13 min. Total time: 23 min.

My kids get frustrated with flaky fish that's hard to pick up with a fork. As a result most of it stays on their plates. So I cut a 1-inch-thick fillet of fish into nuggets that are coated and baked. Then, the kids can dip and pop them into their mouths—no utensils required. Offer ketchup and honey mustard for dipping.

1 pound cod or other lean white fish fillets (about 1 inch thick)
1 large egg
1 large egg white
⅓ cup whole-wheat panko (Japanese breadcrumbs)
2 tablespoons flaxseed meal
¼ teaspoon salt
¼ teaspoon freshly ground black pepper
½ cup ounces all-purpose flour
½ teaspoon garlic powder
Cooking spray

1. Preheat oven to 450°. Cut fish into 24 (1-inch) pieces.

2. Combine egg and egg white in a small bowl; stir well with a whisk. Combine panko and flaxseed meal in a shallow dish. Sprinkle fish with salt and pepper.

3. Combine flour and garlic powder in a large zip-top plastic bag; add fish pieces. Seal bag, and shake to coat fish with flour mixture. Remove fish from bag; discard flour mixture. Dip fish pieces into egg; dredge in panko mixture.

4. Place fish nuggets on a wire rack coated with cooking spray; place rack in a foil-lined jelly-roll pan. Coat fish with cooking spray. Bake at 450° for 10 minutes or until fish flakes easily when tested with a fork.

SERVES 4 (serving size: 6 nuggets)

CALORIES 174; **FAT** 3.7g (sat 0.4g, mono 0.6g, poly 1.4g); **PROTEIN** 23.9g; **CARB** 10.6g; **FIBER** 1.9g; **CHOL** 72mg; **IRON** 1.1mg; **SODIUM** 233mg; **CALC** 24mg

T-Riffic Tilapia Tacos

Hands-on time: 19 min. Total time: 28 min.

For some kids, fish can be a tough sell. But rolled up in a corn tortilla? That changes everything.

¼ cup sliced green onions
¼ cup chopped fresh cilantro
3 tablespoons canola mayonnaise
3 tablespoons reduced-fat sour cream
1 teaspoon grated lime rind
1½ teaspoons fresh lime juice
¼ teaspoon salt
1 garlic clove, minced
1 teaspoon ground cumin
1 teaspoon ground coriander
½ teaspoon Spanish smoked paprika

¼ teaspoon ground red pepper
⅛ teaspoon salt
⅛ teaspoon garlic powder
1½ pounds tilapia fillets
Cooking spray
8 (6-inch) corn tortillas
2 cups angel hair slaw
1 cup chopped tomatoes
½ cup sliced red onion
¼ cup sliced green onions
Chopped fresh cilantro (optional)
Lime wedges

1. Preheat oven to 425°.

2. Combine first 8 ingredients in a small bowl; stir well. Cover and chill.

3. Combine cumin and next 5 ingredients (through garlic powder) in a small bowl; sprinkle spice mixture over both sides of fillets. Place fillets on a baking sheet coated with cooking spray. Bake at 425° for 9 to 10 minutes or until fish flakes easily when tested with a fork. Cool slightly. Place fish in a large bowl; break into pieces with 2 forks.

4. Warm tortillas according to package directions. Place 2 tortillas on each of 4 plates. Arrange ¼ cup slaw on each tortilla. Divide fish among tortillas. Top each tortilla with 2 tablespoons tomato, 1 tablespoon red onion, 1½ teaspoons green onions, and about 1½ tablespoons lime mayonnaise mixture. Garnish with cilantro, if desired. Serve with lime wedges.

SERVES 4 (serving size: 2 tacos)

CALORIES 351; FAT 9.5g (sat 2.1g, mono 2.9g, poly 2.4g); PROTEIN 38.6g; CARB 28.9g; FIBER 5.4g; CHOL 91mg; IRON 2.2mg; SODIUM 435mg; CALC 113mg

SMART STRATEGY

Create a dinner bar. Kids are simply more receptive to food when it's deconstructed—separated out into individual parts rather than piled on a plate together. That's why divided plates are so popular among the kid-set. Consider making a dinner bar, and let everyone happily fill their plate. Here are some ideas:

- *Burrito Bar (tortillas, meat, beans, cheese, salsa, lettuce, tomatoes, and guacamole)*

- *Salad Bar (chopped veggies, seeds, fruit, croutons, cheese, nuts, and hard-cooked eggs)*

- *Pasta Bar (pasta, marinara sauce, chicken, Parmesan cheese, veggies)*

- *Pizza Bar (individual crusts, pizza sauce, veggies, cheeses, meat, pineapple, and spices)*

Yankee Pot Roast

Hands-on time: 18 min. Total time: 3 hr. 55 min.

Pot roast is a family favorite, so I've made a lot of them. But this one, which cooks for hours in a rich, tomato broth, was voted the most tender and juicy.

2 teaspoons olive oil
1 (4-pound) boneless chuck
   roast, trimmed
1 tablespoon kosher salt
1 tablespoon cracked black
   pepper
2 cups coarsely chopped
   onion
2 cups lower-sodium beef
   broth
¼ cup ketchup

2 tablespoons
   Worcestershire sauce
1 cup chopped plum tomato
1¼ pounds small red
   potatoes, quartered
1 pound carrots, peeled and
   cut into 1-inch pieces
2 tablespoons fresh lemon
   juice
Chopped fresh parsley
   (optional)

1. Preheat oven to 300°.

2. Heat a large Dutch oven over medium-high heat. Add olive oil to pan; swirl to coat. Sprinkle roast with salt and pepper. Add roast to pan, browning on all sides (about 8 minutes). Remove from pan. Add onion to pan; sauté 8 minutes or until browned. Return roast to pan. Combine broth, ketchup, and Worcestershire sauce in a small bowl; pour over roast. Add tomato; bring to a simmer.

3. Cover and bake at 300° for 2½ hours or until tender. Add potatoes and carrots; cover and bake an additional 30 minutes or until vegetables are tender. Stir in lemon juice. Garnish with parsley, if desired.

SERVES 10 (serving size: 3 ounces beef and about ½ cup vegetables)

CALORIES 290; **FAT** 8.4g (sat 2.8g, mono 3.7g, poly 0.5g); **PROTEIN** 32.9g; **CARB** 20g; **FIBER** 3g; **CHOL** 92mg; **IRON** 4.3mg; **SODIUM** 756mg; **CALC** 36mg

If you don't have a Dutch oven, use an ovenproof pot and lid. No ovenproof lid? Cover the pot with aluminum foil

Peanutty Stir-Fry

Hands-on time: 18 min. Total time: 38 min.

This stir-fry features sugar snap peas, a crunchy veggie that most kids like. Serve with white or brown rice.

1 (1-pound) flank steak, trimmed

3 tablespoons rice vinegar, divided

2 tablespoons lower-sodium soy sauce, divided

2 teaspoons sugar

2 teaspoons bottled peanut sauce

1/4 teaspoon salt

2 teaspoons dark sesame oil, divided

1 teaspoon refrigerated ginger paste

1/2 teaspoon minced fresh garlic

1 cup broccoli florets

3/4 cup matchstick-cut carrots

1 (8-ounce) package fresh sugar snap peas

1/3 cup chopped green onions

4 teaspoons unsalted, dry-roasted peanuts

1. Place steak in freezer 20 minutes or until firm. Cut steak diagonally across the grain into thin slices.

2. Combine 2 tablespoons vinegar, 1 tablespoon soy sauce, sugar, peanut sauce, and salt in a small bowl; stir with a whisk.

3. Heat a large nonstick skillet over medium-high heat. Add 1 teaspoon oil to pan; swirl to coat. Add steak; stir-fry 3 to 4 minutes. Remove steak from pan with a slotted spoon; place in a bowl, and stir in 1 tablespoon vinegar and 1 tablespoon soy sauce.

4. Wipe pan clean with a paper towel. Heat pan over medium-high heat. Add 1 teaspoon oil; swirl pan to coat. Add ginger paste and garlic; stir-fry 15 seconds. Add broccoli, carrots, and peas; stir-fry 3 minutes. Add steak mixture and peanut sauce mixture; stir-fry 2 minutes or until thoroughly heated. Remove from heat; sprinkle with green onions and peanuts.

SERVES 4 (serving size: 1 1/4 cups)

CALORIES 270; FAT 11.6g (sat 3.5g, mono 4.5g, poly 1.8g); PROTEIN 28.4g; CARB 12.1g; FIBER 3.3g; CHOL 78mg; IRON 3.4mg; SODIUM 582mg; CALC 81mg

REAL MOM, REAL SMART

I have our daughter help prepare dinner, including foods she doesn't like. It seems to help her want to at least try what she helped make. She will take at least one bite, and if she doesn't like it, we discuss what she can do differently next time to make it taste better. I think it makes her feel like a grown-up!

—Qunissa Simpson, San Antonio, TX

Cauliflower popcorn: Toss florets in olive oil and roast on a baking sheet until brown. Toss with kosher salt.

Cheesy roasted broccoli: Try the same method above but use broccoli instead. Sprinkle on some Parmesan cheese a few minutes before the florets are done cooking.

Brown sugar carrots: Cut carrots diagonally into oval slices. Sauté in butter, and sprinkle with a touch of brown sugar.

Crunchy kale or Brussels sprouts chips: Tear kale leaves from hard stems and outer leaves from Brussels sprouts. Drizzle with olive oil, and then sprinkle with salt and the spices of your choosing. Bake until brown and crispy.

Cheesy Mini Meat Loaves

Hands-on time: 11 min. Total time: 46 min.

Your kids may like these little muffins better than a slice of meat loaf, especially if they can leave the fork on the table and eat them out of hand. Serve with mashed potatoes or buttered noodles and a veggie they like.

Cooking spray
1/2 cup finely chopped onion
2 garlic cloves, chopped
3/4 cup quick-cooking oats
2 ounces white cheddar cheese, diced (about 1/2 cup)
1/2 cup ketchup, divided
1/4 cup chopped fresh parsley
2 tablespoons grated fresh Parmesan cheese
1 tablespoon Dijon mustard
1/4 teaspoon salt
1/4 teaspoon dried oregano
1/4 teaspoon freshly ground black pepper
11/2 pounds ground sirloin
1 large egg, lightly beaten
1 tablespoon brown sugar

1. Preheat oven to 425°.

2. Heat a large skillet over medium-high heat. Coat pan with cooking spray. Add onion and garlic; sauté 3 minutes. Combine onion mixture, oats, white cheddar cheese, 1/4 cup ketchup, and next 8 ingredients (through egg) in a bowl; stir gently to combine. Press meat mixture into 12 muffin cups coated with cooking spray.

3. Combine 1/4 cup ketchup and brown sugar in a small bowl; stir well. Spread 1 teaspoon ketchup mixture over each mini meat loaf.

4. Bake at 425° for 25 minutes or until done. Let stand in pan 10 minutes before serving.

SERVES 6 (serving size: 2 mini meat loaves)

CALORIES 306; **FAT** 14.4g (sat 6.2g, mono 4.4g, poly 0.8g); **PROTEIN** 27.9g; **CARB** 16.2g; **FIBER** 1.5g; **CHOL** 112mg; **IRON** 3.3mg; **SODIUM** 532mg; **CALC** 121mg

Peanut Butter–Coconut Chicken Fingers

Hands-on time: 55 min. Total time: 55 min.

A lot of kids love peanut butter, and these crunchy chicken fingers deliver. The recipe's adapted from Brenda Thompson of mealplanningmagic.com—one of my favorite websites for meal planning and recipe ideas. Serve a sweet dipping sauce of orange marmalade, grated lime rind, and grated peeled fresh ginger.

1¼ cups panko (Japanese breadcrumbs)
¼ cup flaked unsweetened coconut
½ teaspoon ground ginger
¼ teaspoon salt
¼ cup light coconut milk

3 tablespoons natural-style peanut butter
2 large egg whites
1 tablespoon water
1½ pounds chicken breast tenders (12 tenders)
2 tablespoons canola oil

Look for flaked unsweetened coconut in the natural foods section of your grocery store.

1. Combine panko, coconut, ginger, and salt in a shallow dish. Combine coconut milk and peanut butter in another shallow dish; stir with a whisk until smooth. Add egg whites and 1 tablespoon water to peanut butter mixture; stir with a whisk until blended.

2. Dip chicken tenders in peanut butter mixture; dredge in panko mixture, pressing to coat.

3. Heat a large nonstick skillet over medium heat. Add 1 tablespoon oil to pan; swirl to coat. Add 6 tenders; cook 8 to 10 minutes on each side or until golden brown and crisp. Repeat procedure with remaining 1 tablespoon oil and 6 tenders.

SERVES 4 (serving size: 3 tenders)

CALORIES 463; **FAT** 20.8g (sat 5.2g, mono 9.0g, poly 4.5g); **PROTEIN** 43.4g; **CARB** 22.8g; **FIBER** 2.2g; **CHOL** 109mg; **IRON** 1mg; **SODIUM** 460mg; **CALC** 11mg

SPEEDY Turkey Burritos

Hands-on time: 26 min. Total time: 31 min.

There's no need for packets of salty taco seasoning mix when you've already got all the raw materials in your pantry. Serve these burritos with a side of black beans or Spanish rice.

Cooking spray
½ cup chopped onion
2 garlic cloves, minced
1 pound ground turkey
  breast
½ cup water
3 tablespoons bottled salsa
2 teaspoons dried oregano
2 teaspoons ground cumin
1½ teaspoons chili powder
1 (4.5-ounce) can chopped
  green chiles, undrained
6 (8-inch) flour tortillas
4 ounces preshredded
  reduced-fat Mexican
  blend cheese (about 1 cup)
Chopped fresh cilantro
  (optional)

1. Heat a large skillet over medium heat. Coat pan with cooking spray. Add onion and garlic to pan, and cook 3 minutes or until tender, stirring frequently. Add ground turkey, and cook 10 minutes or until turkey is browned, stirring to crumble.

2. Add ½ cup water and next 5 ingredients (through green chiles), stirring to combine. Cover pan, and cook 5 minutes over medium heat.

3. Warm tortillas according to package directions. Spoon 2½ tablespoons cheese down center of each tortilla. Top each tortilla with ½ cup turkey mixture; roll up. Garnish with cilantro, if desired.

SERVES 6 (serving size: 1 burrito)

CALORIES 329; **FAT** 11.1g (sat 3.3g, mono 4.2g, poly 2.1g); **PROTEIN** 24.2g;
CARB 32.5g; **FIBER** 4.2g; **CHOL** 63mg; **IRON** 3.2mg; **SODIUM** 513mg; **CALC** 160mg

REAL MOM, REAL SMART

I prepare a seven-day meal plan each week with five prepared meals and two nights of leftovers. I keep a years' worth of past meal plans, so if I run out of ideas or am bored with what we have been eating, I can find inspiration.

—Jennifer Vito, Fort Worth, TX

Super Crunch Chicken Nuggets

Hands-on time: 34 min. Total time: 1 hr. 24 min.

For better or worse, most kids adore chicken nuggets. This version is healthier than the drive-thru kind. Serve baked potato chips—including the plain and sweet potato varieties—and there will be big grins at the table.

1½ pounds skinless, boneless chicken breast, cut into 1-inch pieces
⅓ cup low-fat buttermilk
⅓ cup dill pickle juice
1½ cups panko (Japanese breadcrumbs)
¼ teaspoon kosher salt

2 tablespoons water
1 large egg, lightly beaten
¼ cup canola mayonnaise
¼ cup plain fat-free Greek yogurt
1 tablespoon honey
1 tablespoon yellow mustard
1 teaspoon Dijon mustard

1. Combine first 3 ingredients in a large zip-top plastic bag. Marinate in refrigerator 1 hour, turning occasionally.

2. Heat a large skillet over medium heat. Add panko; cook 3 minutes or until toasted, stirring frequently.

3. Preheat oven to 400°.

4. Remove chicken from marinade; discard marinade. Sprinkle chicken with salt. Place panko in a zip-top plastic bag. Combine 2 tablespoons water and egg in a shallow dish; dip half of chicken in egg mixture. Add chicken to bag; seal and shake to coat. Remove chicken from bag; arrange chicken in a single layer on a baking sheet. Repeat procedure with remaining egg mixture, panko, and chicken. Bake at 400° for 12 minutes or until done.

5. Combine mayonnaise and remaining ingredients in a medium bowl; stir to combine. Serve with chicken nuggets.

SERVES 8 (serving size: about 6 nuggets and 1 tablespoon sauce)

CALORIES 251; **FAT** 105g (sat 1.3g, mono 4.7g, poly 2.1g); **PROTEIN** 21g; **CARB** 18g; **FIBER** 0.1g; **CHOL** 73mg; **IRON** 1mg; **SODIUM** 427mg; **CALC** 28mg

CRAZY TRICK *that actually works!*

Kids are more likely to try food when it's got a fun name like X-Ray Vision Carrots, according to research at Cornell University. "Rebrand" your dinners by giving them names that intrigue your kids or just make them smile. Around here, we have "Daddy's Famous Eggs," "Henry's Favorite Garlic Noodles," and "Barbecue Kitchen Sandwiches." That last recipe got its name when Sam mispronounced "chicken." This still gets a laugh at the dinner table, and sometimes a laugh is exactly what you need to set the right tone at mealtime.

MAKE-AHEAD Creamy Ranch-Style Dip

Hands-on time: 20 min. Total time: 20 min.

Kids eat more vegetables when they're served with dip, but the bottled kind has all sorts of sweeteners, colors, and preservatives. Mix up this version instead.

4 ounces ⅓-less-fat cream cheese, softened (about ½ cup)
3 tablespoons nonfat buttermilk
2 tablespoons chopped fresh flat-leaf parsley
1 teaspoon chopped fresh dill

½ teaspoon minced fresh garlic
¼ teaspoon onion powder
¼ teaspoon salt
¼ teaspoon freshly ground black pepper

1. Combine cream cheese and buttermilk in a small bowl, stirring with a whisk until blended. Stir in remaining ingredients. Serve with fresh vegetables.

SERVES 6 (serving size: 2 tablespoons)

CALORIES 52; FAT 4.3g (sat 2.4g, mono 1.1g, poly 0.2g); PROTEIN 2.1g; CARB 1.4g; FIBER 0.1g; CHOL 14mg; IRON 0.1mg; SODIUM 170mg; CALC 34mg

REAL MOM, REAL SMART

I always let my son have choices when possible, like letting him pick what kind of vegetable we have with dinner. He got a cookbook for his birthday, and every week I let him pick one recipe that I make for dinner.

—Claire Grattan, Hamlin, NY

DINNERTIME SURVIVAL GUIDE TOP 5

TIPS FOR RAISING VEGGIE LOVERS

#1

BE COOL: Pressuring kids to take a bite of a new vegetable can backfire and make them more resistant to trying. Be sure veggies are on the table and casually mention how good they taste to you—but let your child decide if she eats them.

#2

TRY DIFFERENT SHAPES: Sam doesn't like baby carrots but loves when I serve him a whole washed and peeled carrot "like a rabbit." Try celery "moons" if they don't like sticks or pepper rings if they don't like strips. Sounds nuts, but it really can make a difference.

#3

CHANNEL YOUR INNER 10-YEAR-OLD: Would you rather have been served crunchy broccoli sprinkled with cheese or mushy, plain florets? Steam or roast fresh veggies to keep them crisp.

#4

EMBRACE RANCH DRESSING: Kids love to dip—and offering veggies with it may make them seem less intimidating. Don't like the bottled kind? Try the easy DIY version on page 126.

#5

STRIKE WHILE THE KID IS HUNGRY: My "only veggies in the hour before dinner" rule has been very successful at increasing kids' veggie intake, ensuring they're still hungry when they come to the dinner table.

Zesty Lemon Waffles with Blueberries

Hands-on time: 48 min. Total time: 48 min.

Brinner (aka breakfast for dinner) is one meal when I can guarantee that everyone at the table is pleased— and licking their plates clean. Stack leftover waffles between sheets of wax paper, and freeze in an airtight container. Pop in the toaster for a quick breakfast.

4.75 ounces whole-wheat flour (about 1 cup)
4.5 ounces all-purpose flour (about 1 cup)
6 tablespoons flaxseed meal
2 tablespoons sugar
1 tablespoon baking powder
$3/4$ teaspoon baking soda
$1/4$ teaspoon salt
1 cup fat-free milk
1 cup plain fat-free yogurt

2 tablespoons butter, melted
4 large eggs, lightly beaten
$1^1/2$ teaspoons grated lemon rind
1 tablespoon fresh lemon juice
Cooking spray
$2^1/2$ cups blueberries
$1^1/4$ cups maple syrup
Grated lemon rind (optional)

1. Weigh or lightly spoon flours into dry measuring cups; level with a knife. Combine flours and next 5 ingredients (through salt) in a large bowl; stir well. Combine milk, yogurt, melted butter, and eggs; add to flour mixture, stirring until smooth. Stir in lemon rind and juice.

2. Coat a Belgian waffle iron with cooking spray; preheat. Spoon about $1/2$ cup batter per 4-inch waffle onto hot waffle iron, spreading batter to edges. Cook 4 to 6 minutes or until steaming stops; repeat procedure with remaining batter. Serve waffles with blueberries and syrup. Garnish with lemon rind, if desired.

SERVES 10 (serving size: 1 waffle, $1/4$ cup blueberries, and 2 tablespoons syrup)

CALORIES 323; **FAT** 6.9g (sat 2.2g, mono 1.7g, poly 1.9g); **PROTEIN** 9.3g; **CARB** 59.3g; **FIBER** 3.9g; **CHOL** 82mg; **IRON** 1.7mg; **SODIUM** 389mg; **CALC** 216mg

Look for pure or natural maple syrup. "Pancake syrup" often contains no actual maple syrup at all.

Roasted Cauliflower with Sage

Hands-on time: 7 min. Total time: 18 min.

Roasting actually caramelizes the natural sugars in cauliflower, bringing out just a touch of sweetness.

1 (1¾-pound) head cauliflower, trimmed and cut into 1½-inch florets
1 tablespoon olive oil
½ teaspoon freshly ground black pepper
¼ teaspoon salt
2 tablespoons fresh sage leaves
2 teaspoons grated lemon rind

1. Preheat oven to 500°.

2. Place a large baking sheet in oven. Heat 5 minutes.

3. While pan heats, place cauliflower in a large bowl. Drizzle cauliflower with oil; toss until coated. Sprinkle with pepper and salt; toss well. Spread cauliflower in a single layer on hot pan.

4. Bake at 500° for 12 minutes or until browned and tender. Transfer cauliflower to a bowl. Add sage and lemon rind; toss well. Serve immediately.

SERVES 6 (serving size: ¾ cup)

CALORIES 55; **FAT** 2.4g (sat 0.3g, mono 1.7g, poly 0.3g); **PROTEIN** 2.7g; **CARB** 7.3g; **FIBER** 3.4g; **CHOL** 0mg; **IRON** 0.6mg; **SODIUM** 138mg; **CALC** 35mg

If you don't have sage, try rosemary instead.

EASY Roasted Green Beans

Hands-on time: 10 min. Total time: 35 min.

Soggy, mushy veggies are a kid's worst enemy. But roasting gives everything a crispiness they'll love. Green beans, a familiar favorite, work great with this cooking technique.

1 tablespoon olive oil
¼ teaspoon salt
¼ teaspoon freshly ground
   black pepper

10 ounces trimmed French
   green beans
2 garlic cloves, thinly sliced
Cooking spray

1. Preheat oven to 425°.

2. Combine olive oil, salt, black pepper, green beans, and garlic on a jelly-roll pan coated with cooking spray; toss to coat.

3. Place pan on bottom rack in oven. Bake at 425° for 25 minutes, stirring once.

SERVES 4 (serving size: 1 cup)

CALORIES 141; FAT 4.3g (sat 0.6g, mono 2.9g, poly 0.6g); PROTEIN 3.6g; CARB 24.2g; FIBER 4.2g; CHOL 0mg; IRON 1.3mg; SODIUM 169mg; CALC 45mg

SMART STRATEGY

Disband the Clean Plate Club. *Frustrated when your child leaves just a few little bites on his plate? It's tempting to ask him to finish, but resist: According to research, preschool children who were forced to finish their meals ate 41 percent more at daycare, possibly because not being in control of how much they eat disrupts their ability to regulate their own food intake.*

Salted Caramel Brownies

Hands-on time: 30 min. Total time: 1 hr. 15 min.

Everyone will swoon over these rich little dessert bars.

Brownies:
3.4 ounces all-purpose flour
  (about ¾ cup)
1 cup granulated sugar
¾ cup unsweetened cocoa
½ cup packed brown sugar
½ teaspoon baking powder
6 tablespoons butter, melted
1 teaspoon vanilla extract
2 large eggs, lightly beaten
Cooking spray

Topping:
¼ cup butter
¼ cup packed brown sugar
3½ tablespoons evaporated
  fat-free milk, divided
½ cup powdered sugar
¼ teaspoon vanilla extract
1 ounce bittersweet
  chocolate, coarsely
  chopped
⅛ teaspoon coarse sea salt

1. Preheat oven to 350°.

2. To prepare brownies, weigh or lightly spoon flour into dry measuring cups; level with a knife. Combine flour and next 4 ingredients (through baking powder) in a large bowl, stirring well with a whisk. Combine 6 tablespoons butter, 1 teaspoon vanilla, and eggs. Add butter mixture to flour mixture; stir to combine. Scrape batter into a 9-inch square metal baking pan lightly coated with cooking spray. Bake at 350° for 19 minutes or until a wooden pick inserted in center comes out with moist crumbs clinging. Cool in pan on a wire rack.

3. To prepare topping, melt ¼ cup butter in a saucepan over medium heat. Add ¼ cup brown sugar and 1½ tablespoons milk; cook 2 minutes. Remove from heat. Add powdered sugar and ¼ teaspoon vanilla; stir with a whisk until smooth. Spread mixture over cooled brownies. Let stand 20 minutes or until set.

4. Combine 2 tablespoons milk and chocolate in a microwave-safe bowl; microwave at HIGH 45 seconds or until melted, stirring after 20 seconds. Stir just until smooth; drizzle over caramel. Sprinkle with sea salt; let stand until set. Cut into bars.

SERVES 20 (serving size: 1 brownie)

CALORIES 180; **FAT** 7.2g (sat 4.1g, mono 1.7g, poly 0.3g); **PROTEIN** 2.1g; **CARB** 27.8g; **FIBER** 0.8g; **CHOL** 37mg; **IRON** 0.9mg; **SODIUM** 76mg; **CALC** 26mg

CRAZY TRICK
that actually works!

Serve dessert with dinner—especially if your kids seem fixated on dessert (racing through their meal to get to the sweets or asking "How many bites do I have to eat to get a cookie?"). Allow them to have dessert on their plate along with everything else (in a small portion that won't fill them up). Chances are, they'll eat it first, and then move on to their other food.

NOBODY'S AROUND TO EAT IT ANYWAY

Adaptable Meals for Hectic Schedules

"Family dinner" has such a quaint, *Leave It to Beaver* sound to it, doesn't it? But as you probably know by now, the reality is much different. There are spouses who don't get home from work until 8 p.m. and toddlers who fall asleep at the dinner table at 5:30. There are evening softball practices and piano lessons—with you on minivan shuttle service. You may be wondering if it's even worth trying to wrangle the family together for dinner. It is.

Research has shown time and again that kids who eat dinner with their families are better off emotionally, socially, and nutritionally. They eat more vegetables and fruits, achieve more in school, and are less likely to dabble in drugs and alcohol. **And we don't need science to tell us that the drive-thru's got nothing on a home-cooked meal.**

GET A GAME PLAN.

If eating dinner as a family feels like mission impossible, you're likely facing one of three common dilemmas, or maybe you've got all of these happening in the same week—lucky you!

THE SCENARIO	THE SOLUTION
Between the time everyone gets home from school and the time everyone is out the door to evening activities, you've got exactly 28 minutes to make and eat dinner.	A meal in the slow cooker (such as **Slow-Cooker Sweet Glazed Chicken Thighs,** page 140), a really fast dish (like **Speedy Sloppy Joe Sliders,** page 149), or cold salads from the fridge (such as **Black Bean Taco Salad with Lime Vinaigrette,** page 167).
Jobs and school bleed into evening activities, and you're only home long enough to grab your son's violin and daughter's shin guards.	A family tailgate at the soccer field or ballet-school parking lot. Pack up dinner the night before or that morning, either in portable dishes or individual divided containers. One possible menu: **Grilled Veggie and Hummus Wraps** (page 150), **Sweet-Tart Kale Salad** (page 151), and **Marbled Chocolate-Banana Bread** (page 153). (Or PB&Js—I don't judge.)
Everyone is home and hungry at completely different times.	Dinners that can be held on "warm" in the slow cooker and eaten in shifts, like **Make-Ahead Beef-Barley Soup** (page 146); dishes that can be reheated, like **Slow-Roasted Pulled Pork** (page 138); or meals that older kids and spouses can pull out of the fridge or freezer and cook themselves. For that scenario, I love **Sausage and Pepper Calzones** (page 144).

(Continued)

MAKE YOUR DINNER TABLE A HAPPY PLACE.

When it comes to family dinner, quality trumps quantity any day of the week. If you create a warm, welcoming environment at the table, your family will want to be there. That's especially important for teens (and even spouses) who may have some choice in whether or not they're home in time for dinner. For younger kids, a pleasant mealtime means better behavior—and maybe even fewer "yucks," too. Here are some pointers:

DO	DON'T
Make sure there's a favorite on the table. If your child isn't a huge fan of the main dish, offer a bowl of fruit or a basket of bread that will be familiar and filling.	**Nag about homework.** Or the trash they didn't take out. Or the vegetables they aren't eating. Keep the vibe positive and take those 15 to 30 minutes to simply enjoy each other.
Ask specific, open-ended questions. Instead of "Did you have a good day at school?" ask "What are you working on in art class?"	**Be a short-order cook.** Making five different meals only adds to your mealtime stress.
Play games. Have everyone share a story about the funniest thing they saw that day or list their desert-island-top-five foods. Or write down a bunch of questions (some serious, some silly), stick them in a jar, and take turns picking one out every night.	**Allow technology at the table.** Text messages, phone calls, and Facebook can wait.

Reclaim family dinner.

Crazy but true: Dinner may be the only time of the day when everyone in the family is in the same room, sitting together. That's valuable stuff. "Family dinner is good for family culture," says Grace Freedman, PhD, a mom of three who promotes family dinner through advocacy and research. "I have a good relationship with my kids, and I think, in part, that's because we have a ritual of family dinner." She has these tips on making it happen:

Be honest with yourself. When you have family members going in all different directions—work, the gym, sports practices, lessons—it's not realistic to plan for nightly 6 p.m. family dinners. But two nights a week at 7 p.m. plus a weekly Sunday dinner might work. Aim for at least three family dinners a week if you can—that's the frequency that seems to show a benefit for kids, according to researchers at Cornell University.

Call a family meeting. Let everyone know the dinner schedule. Make it clear why family dinner is important and that you expect everyone to be there. Having a firm day and time gives working parents an incentive to get home.

Embrace the chaos. Family dinner won't be perfect. There will be spilled glasses, finicky eaters, and grumpy moods. There will be nights when all you can manage are grilled cheese sandwiches. There will also be basketball tournaments that will throw a monkey wrench into everything. Focus on the fact that you're trying—and that most weeks, you're doing okay.

Give everyone a job. When everyone chips in, they feel invested in mealtime and a part of something larger. Even small children can put placemats on the table or clear everyone's napkins. Older kids can even take charge of cooking dinner once a week.

Slow-Roasted Pulled Pork

Hands-on time: 40 min. Total time: 9 hr. 50 min.

While the pork bakes several hours unattended, take a load off. Or do laundry. Your call.

5 tablespoons dark brown sugar, divided
1 tablespoon plus 2 teaspoons smoked paprika, divided
1 tablespoon plus 1 teaspoon chili powder, divided
2 teaspoons ground cumin
1 teaspoon salt
1 teaspoon black pepper
½ teaspoon dry mustard
½ teaspoon ground chipotle chile pepper
1 (5-pound) boneless pork shoulder (Boston butt), trimmed
Cooking spray
2 cups water, divided
1¼ cups cider vinegar, divided
1 cup ketchup, divided

1. To prepare pork, combine 2 tablespoons sugar, 1 tablespoon paprika, 1 tablespoon chili powder, cumin, and next 4 ingredients; rub sugar mixture over pork. Let pork stand at room temperature 1 hour.

2. Preheat oven to 225°. Place pork on rack of a roasting pan coated with cooking spray. Pour 1 cup water in bottom of pan. Place rack in pan. Bake at 225° for 1 hour.

3. Combine ½ cup vinegar and ¼ cup ketchup in a medium bowl; brush pork with ketchup mixture (do not remove from oven). Bake an additional 3 hours, basting every hour with ketchup mixture.

4. Pour 1 cup water in bottom of roasting pan. Cover pork and pan tightly with foil. Bake an additional 3 hours and 45 minutes or until a thermometer registers 190°. Remove from oven; let stand, covered, 45 minutes.

Make a double batch of the sauce to drizzle on leftovers.

5. To prepare sauce, combine ¾ cup vinegar, ¾ cup ketchup, 3 tablespoons sugar, 2 teaspoons paprika, and 1 teaspoon chili powder in a small saucepan. Bring to a boil over medium-high heat, stirring occasionally with a whisk. Boil 5 minutes or until slightly thick. Shred pork with 2 forks, and serve with sauce.

SERVES 16 (serving size: about 3 ounces pork and 1 tablespoon sauce)

CALORIES 283; **FAT** 15.4g (sat 5.5g, mono 6.8g, poly 1.5g); **PROTEIN** 26.2g; **CARB** 8.1g; **FIBER** 0.4g; **CHOL** 90mg; **IRON** 2.1mg; **SODIUM** 402mg; **CALC** 40mg

Pistachio Pesto Pasta

Hands-on time: 17 min. Total time: 17 min.

Toss hot, cooked fusilli with a homemade pistachio pesto for a refreshing twist on traditional pine nut–based pesto dishes. Fresh lemon juice lends a great flavor boost. This main dish is best served immediately after tossing, so reserve the pasta and pesto separately for latecomers to toss themselves.

2 (6-ounce) skinless, boneless chicken breast halves
1/2 teaspoon salt, divided
1/4 teaspoon freshly ground black pepper
Cooking spray
8 ounces uncooked fusilli (short twisted pasta)
2 garlic cloves

2 cups basil leaves
1/4 cup shelled dry-roasted pistachios
2 tablespoons fresh lemon juice
1 1/2 tablespoons extra-virgin olive oil
1 ounce grated Parmesan cheese (about 1/4 cup)

1. Preheat grill to medium-high heat.

2. Sprinkle chicken with 1/4 teaspoon salt and pepper. Place chicken on grill rack coated with cooking spray; grill 5 minutes on each side or until done. Let stand 5 minutes; slice chicken into 1/2-inch-thick strips.

3. Cook pasta according to package directions, omitting salt and fat. Drain pasta, reserving 1/4 cup cooking liquid.

4. Drop garlic through food chute with food processor on; process until minced. Add 1/4 teaspoon salt, basil, pistachios, lemon juice, and oil; process until smooth, scraping sides of bowl once. Transfer pesto to a large bowl; stir in reserved 1/4 cup pasta water and cheese. Add chicken and pasta; toss gently to coat.

SERVES 4 (serving size: 1 1/3 cups)

CALORIES 434; **FAT** 14.1g (sat 3g, mono 6.7g, poly 2g); **PROTEIN** 30.7g; **CARB** 46.4g; **FIBER** 3g; **CHOL** 59mg; **IRON** 3.3mg; **SODIUM** 512mg; **CALC** 148mg

SMART STRATEGY

Eat early. Early-bird-special early. Kids are frequently famished roughly an hour or so before dinnertime, creating the universal dilemma: Feed them a snack, and they'll be too full for your home-cooked meal, or don't feed them and risk a potential dinner-ruining meltdown. So instead of fighting against that 4 o'clock hunger, embrace it. When possible, move dinner to 4 p.m. Then, after you get your kids to bed, have a light snack or some leftovers if you're still hungry. If you have teenagers, a substantial 4 p.m. snack and a later mealtime might work better.

SLOW-COOKER Sweet Glazed Chicken Thighs

Hands-on time: 15 min. Total time: 2 hr. 45 min.

Soccer moms, rejoice: Turn on the slow cooker before you head out for evening activities, and dinner will be ready when you get home.

2 pounds skinless, boneless chicken thighs
1/2 teaspoon freshly ground black pepper
1/4 teaspoon salt
1 teaspoon olive oil
Cooking spray
1 cup pineapple juice

2 tablespoons brown sugar
2 tablespoons lower-sodium soy sauce
3 tablespoons water
2 tablespoons cornstarch
3 cups hot cooked rice
3 tablespoons diagonally sliced green onions

1. Sprinkle chicken with pepper and salt. Heat a large nonstick skillet over medium-high heat. Add oil to pan; swirl to coat. Add chicken to pan. Cook 2 to 3 minutes on each side or until browned. Transfer chicken to a 4-quart electric slow cooker coated with cooking spray. Stir pineapple juice into drippings, scraping pan to loosen browned bits. Remove from heat; stir in brown sugar and soy sauce. Pour juice mixture over chicken. Cover and cook on LOW for 2 1/2 hours.

2. Transfer chicken to a serving platter with a slotted spoon. Increase heat to HIGH. Combine 3 tablespoons water and cornstarch in a small bowl; add to sauce in slow cooker, stirring with a whisk. Cook 2 minutes or until sauce thickens, stirring constantly with whisk.

3. Place rice on each of 6 plates. Top with chicken thighs and sauce. Sprinkle each serving with green onions.

SERVES 6 (serving size: 1/2 cup rice, 1 chicken thigh, about 1/3 cup sauce, and 1 1/2 teaspoons green onions)

CALORIES 339; **FAT** 7.1g (sat 1.7g, mono 2.5g, poly 1.6g); **PROTEIN** 32.4g; **CARB** 33.7g; **FIBER** 0.6g; **CHOL** 125mg; **IRON** 2.8mg; **SODIUM** 363mg; **CALC** 35mg

CRAZY TRICK
that actually works!

Get your slow cooker off the basement shelf and onto your counter—and keep it there. Sounds silly, but eliminating the step of hauling it out and setting it up means you're more likely to use it. And after your meal is cooked, you can use the "warm" setting for hours if family members are eating in shifts.

Spinach Meatballs and Spaghetti

Hands-on time: 25 min. Total time: 35 min.

This recipe is adapted from Brianne DeRosa, author of the blog redroundorgreen.com. I make this recipe through step 2 when I have some free time, and pop the meatballs and sauce in the freezer. Then, on a busy night, all we do is defrost the meatballs and get them hot in the microwave while we cook the spaghetti.

1 pound ground turkey breast

3 cups bagged prewashed spinach, finely chopped

1 cup quick-cooking oats

2 ounces finely shredded fresh Parmesan cheese (about ½ cup)

½ cup diced onion

1 teaspoon dried Italian seasoning

1 teaspoon bottled minced garlic

½ teaspoon salt

½ teaspoon freshly ground black pepper

2 large eggs

2 tablespoons olive oil

1½ cups family marinara organic pasta sauce (such as Amy's)

8 ounces uncooked spaghetti

2 tablespoons finely shredded Parmesan cheese

1. Combine first 10 ingredients in a bowl; shape into 12 (1-inch) meatballs.

2. Heat a large nonstick skillet over medium-high heat. Add oil to pan; swirl to coat. Add meatballs; cook 8 minutes, browning on all sides. Reduce heat to medium; add marinara sauce. Cook 4 minutes or until meatballs are done, stirring occasionally.

3. Cook spaghetti according to package directions, omitting salt and fat. Serve meatballs and sauce over spaghetti; sprinkle with cheese.

SERVES 4 (serving size: 3 meatballs, ½ cup sauce, and 1½ teaspoons cheese)

CALORIES 429; **FAT** 17.7g (sat 4.9, mono 7.7g, poly 1.9g); **PROTEIN** 42.1g; **CARB** 27.8g; **FIBER** 6.1g; **CHOL** 153mg; **IRON** 4.6mg; **SODIUM** 1132mg; **CALC** 239mg

REAL MOM, REAL SMART

I started a tradition when the kids were little of eating a "fancy" dinner in the dining room on Sundays with candles, placemats, and nice plates. We still eat together on Sundays, usually a more elaborate meal and sometimes in the dining room. It still feels special and for some reason we have great family conversations in there.

—Jill Castle, RD, justtherightbyte.com

Sausage and Pepper Calzones

Hands-on time: 37 min. Total time: 2 hr. 31 min.

Make these on the weekend, and you can pull them out of the freezer and pop them right into the oven whenever you need a fast meal. Feel free to customize the fillings, too. Substitute ingredients like turkey pepperoni, spinach, feta, chopped tomato, and leftover chicken or steak for some of the ingredients below.

Dough:
12.3 ounces all-purpose flour, divided (about 2¾ cups)
1 cup warm water (100° to 110°)
1 package dry yeast (about 2¼ teaspoons)
Dash of sugar
1 tablespoon extra-virgin olive oil
¾ teaspoon kosher salt
Cooking spray

Filling:
1 teaspoon extra-virgin olive oil
1 pound chicken apple sausage (such as Gerhard's), cut into ¼-inch slices
2 cups thinly sliced red bell pepper (about 2)
1 cup chopped onion
2 garlic cloves, minced
3 ounces shredded part-skim mozzarella cheese (about ¾ cup)
½ cup unsalted tomato sauce
¼ cup 2% low-fat cottage cheese
2 tablespoons grated fresh Parmesan cheese
1 teaspoon dried oregano
½ teaspoon kosher salt
¼ teaspoon crushed red pepper

1. To prepare dough, weigh or lightly spoon flour into dry measuring cups; level with a knife. Combine 2.2 ounces flour (about 1/2 cup), 1 cup warm water, yeast, and sugar in a large bowl; let stand 15 minutes. Gradually add 7.9 ounces flour (about 1 3/4 cups), 1 tablespoon oil, and 3/4 teaspoon salt; stir until a soft dough forms. Knead until smooth and elastic (about 8 minutes); add as much as 1/2 cup flour, 1 tablespoon at a time, to prevent dough from sticking to hands.

2. Place dough in a large bowl coated with cooking spray, turning to coat top. Cover and let rise in a warm place (85°), free from drafts, 1 hour or until doubled in size. (Gently press two fingers into dough. If indentation remains, dough has risen enough.)

3. To prepare filling, heat a large nonstick skillet over medium-high heat. Add 1 teaspoon oil to pan; swirl to coat. Add sausage, bell pepper, onion, and garlic; sauté 10 minutes or until tender. Spoon mixture into a bowl; cool slightly. Add mozzarella and remaining ingredients to sausage mixture; stir well.

4. Preheat oven to 450°.

5. Punch dough down; cover and let rest 5 minutes. Divide into 8 equal portions. Roll each portion into a 6-inch circle on a lightly floured surface. Spoon about 1/2 cup sausage mixture onto half of each circle, leaving a 1/2-inch border. Fold dough over filling; crimp edges of dough with fingers to seal. Place calzones on a large baking sheet lined with foil and coated with cooking spray. Pierce tops of dough once with a fork. Lightly coat calzones with cooking spray. Bake at 450° for 14 minutes or until browned. Remove from oven. Cool completely on a wire rack.

6. Coat a sheet of foil with cooking spray. Place 1 calzone on coated side of foil; seal. Repeat procedure with remaining calzones and cooking spray. Place calzones in a heavy-duty zip-top plastic bag; freeze.

7. To reheat calzones, preheat oven to 450°.

8. Place foil-wrapped, frozen calzones on a large baking sheet. Bake at 450° for 40 minutes or until thoroughly heated.

SERVES 8 (serving size: 1 calzone)

CALORIES 327; **FAT** 10.7g (sat 3.5g, mono 2.4g, poly 0.6g); **PROTEIN** 16.3g; **CARB** 42g; **FIBER** 4g; **CHOL** 49mg; **IRON** 3.2mg; **SODIUM** 680mg; **CALC** 124mg

REAL MOM, REAL SMART

We pack bento-style meals in advance and have picnics out of the trunk of our station wagon. Usually it's cold foods like salads, sandwiches, and fruit, but sometimes I pack stews, soups, or chili in a thermos.

—Kathleen Yoneyama, Rocky Point, NY

MAKE-AHEAD
Beef-Barley Soup

Hands-on time: 13 min. Total time: 2 hr. 23 min.

This is one of my favorite Cooking Light soups. I customize it for my kids: My older son likes lots of meat in his dish; my younger one prefers a small bowl of just broth and meat on the side. Since it means I'm still only cooking one meal, I don't mind.

Cooking spray
3/4 pound boneless chuck
   roast, trimmed and cut
   into 1/2-inch pieces
1 1/2 cups thinly sliced carrot
1 1/2 cups thinly sliced celery
2/3 cup chopped onion
1 (8-ounce) package
   presliced mushrooms

4 cups fat-free, lower-sodium
   beef broth
1 bay leaf
2/3 cup uncooked pearl
   barley
1/2 teaspoon salt
1/2 teaspoon freshly ground
   black pepper

1. Heat a Dutch oven over medium-high heat. Coat pan with cooking spray. Add beef to pan; cook 4 minutes or until browned, stirring frequently. Remove beef from pan.

2. Add carrot, celery, onion, and mushrooms to pan; cook 6 minutes or until liquid almost evaporates. Add beef, broth, and bay leaf. Bring to a simmer over medium-high heat. Cover, reduce heat, and simmer 1 1/2 hours or until beef is tender, stirring occasionally.

If you don't have pearl barley, use rice instead.

3. Stir in barley; cover and simmer 30 minutes or until barley is tender. Stir in salt and pepper. Discard bay leaf.

SERVES 4 (serving size: 2 cups)

CALORIES 341; FAT 11.4g (sat 4.3g, mono 4.6g, poly 0.8g); PROTEIN 24.1g; CARB 36.2g; FIBER 8.2g; CHOL 53mg; IRON 2.8mg; SODIUM 837mg; CALC 61mg

DINNERTIME SURVIVAL GUIDE TOP 5 | THINGS TO NEVER SAY AT DINNER

#1
"YOU HAVE TO TRY IT."
This may work for some kids but can seriously backfire with others (like my stubborn Sam), causing dinnertime stand-offs and a negative vibe at the table.

#2
"YOU WOULDN'T LIKE IT."
I may warn my kids about a spicy dish, but I'd never discourage them from trying something—even if I think they're going to hate it.

#3
"JUST TWO MORE BITES."
I was guilty of this bites-bargaining when my kids were younger. But no more. Asking kids to eat a certain amount of food isn't fair and doesn't help them self-regulate.

#4
"NO DESSERT UNTIL YOU FINISH YOUR VEGGIES."
Making dessert a reward for eating "healthy food" elevates sweets to extra-special status (and kids are liable to rush through dinner to get it).

#5
"YOU'RE SUCH A PICKY EATER." It's not helpful to label kids in this way, and it doesn't encourage them to branch out.

Out-n-In California Burger

Hands-on time: 22 min. Total time: 22 min.

When you give your family a heads-up that you're serving these, they may just rearrange their schedules to be home on time.

3 tablespoons ketchup
2 tablespoons canola
  mayonnaise
2 teaspoons sweet pickle
  relish
1 teaspoon Dijon mustard
1 pound ground sirloin
1/8 teaspoon salt
1/8 teaspoon freshly ground
  black pepper
Cooking spray
4 green leaf lettuce leaves

4 (1 1/2-ounce) hamburger
  buns
8 (1/4-inch-thick) slices
  tomato
1/2 ripe peeled avocado, cut
  into 1/8-inch-thick slices
4 (1/4-inch-thick) slices
  red onion, separated into
  rings
8 bread-and-butter pickle
  chips

1. Combine first 4 ingredients in a small bowl.

2. Divide beef into 4 equal portions, gently shaping each into a 1/2-inch-thick patty. Press a nickel-sized indentation in center of each patty; sprinkle patties with salt and pepper. Heat a large skillet or grill pan over medium-high heat. Coat pan with cooking spray. Add patties to pan; cook 3 minutes on each side or until desired degree of doneness.

3. Place 1 lettuce leaf on bottom half of each hamburger bun; top with 2 tomato slices, 1 patty, about 2 avocado slices, about 2 onion rings, 2 pickle chips, about 1 1/2 tablespoons sauce, and top half of bun.

SERVES 4 (serving size: 1 burger)

CALORIES 371; FAT 14.7g (sat 3.2g, mono 7g, poly 3g); PROTEIN 27.4g; CARB 33.1g; FIBER 2.8g; CHOL 63mg; IRON 3.7mg; SODIUM 766mg; CALC 91mg

SPEEDY Sloppy Joe Sliders

Hands-on time: 17 min. Total time: 17 min.

This skillet meal comes together quickly on a busy weeknight, and the carrot is a nearly invisible little boost of nutrition. Slider buns are the perfect size for little hands. The beef mixture can be tossed into a slow cooker to stay warm, and it reheats well, too.

1 large carrot
³/₄ cup chopped onion
10 ounces lean ground beef
1 teaspoon garlic powder
1 teaspoon chili powder
¹/₄ teaspoon freshly ground black pepper
¹/₄ cup ketchup
1 tablespoon Dijon mustard
1 tablespoon Worcestershire sauce
1 tablespoon tomato paste
1 teaspoon red wine vinegar
1 (8-ounce) can unsalted tomato sauce
8 (1¹/₄-ounce) slider hamburger buns

1. Preheat broiler.

2. Heat a large nonstick skillet over medium-high heat. While pan is heating, grate carrot. Add carrot, onion, and beef to pan; cook 6 minutes or until beef is browned and vegetables are tender. Add garlic powder, chili powder, and pepper; cook 1 minute.

3. Combine ¹/₄ cup ketchup and next 5 ingredients (through tomato sauce) in a small bowl. Add ketchup mixture to pan, stirring to coat beef mixture. Simmer 5 minutes or until thick, stirring occasionally.

4. While sauce thickens, arrange buns, cut sides up, in a single layer on a baking sheet. Broil 2 minutes or until lightly toasted. Place about ¹/₄ cup beef mixture on bottom half of each bun; top each slider with top half of bun.

SERVES 4 (serving size: 2 sliders)

CALORIES 373; **FAT** 10g (sat 3.6g, mono 3.5g, poly 2.3g); **PROTEIN** 23.1g; **CARB** 52.2g; **FIBER** 4.2g; **CHOL** 38mg; **IRON** 4mg; **SODIUM** 736mg; **CALC** 111mg

If you don't have tomato sauce, jarred pasta sauce works in a pinch.

Grilled Veggie and Hummus Wraps

Hands-on-time: 22 min. Total time: 22 min.

This is ideal for chaotic evenings because you can assemble the wraps with the warm veggies straight from the grill pan for a hot sandwich—or you can cook the veggies in advance, and store them in the fridge for a cold sandwich.

4 (1/2-inch-thick) slices red onion

1 red bell pepper, seeded and quartered

1 medium eggplant, cut into 1/2-inch-thick slices (about 3/4 pound)

2 tablespoons olive oil, divided

1/4 cup chopped fresh flat-leaf parsley

1/8 teaspoon kosher salt

1 (8-ounce) container plain hummus

4 (1.9-ounce) whole-grain flatbreads (such as Flatout Light)

2 ounces crumbled feta cheese (about 1/2 cup)

1. Heat a large grill pan over medium-high heat. Brush onion, bell pepper, and eggplant with 1 tablespoon oil. Add onion and bell pepper to pan; cook 3 minutes on each side or until grill marks appear. Remove from pan. Add eggplant to pan; cook 3 minutes on each side or until grill marks appear. Remove from pan; coarsely chop vegetables. Combine vegetables, 1 tablespoon oil, parsley, and salt; toss to combine.

2. Spread 1/4 cup hummus over each flatbread, leaving a 1/2-inch border around edges. Divide vegetables over each flatbread; top each with 2 tablespoons cheese. Roll up wraps, and cut in half.

SERVES 4 (serving size: 1 wrap)

CALORIES 356; FAT 22.7g (sat 3.1g, mono 13.6g, poly 4.4g); PROTEIN 16.8g; CARB 35.4g; FIBER 15.3g; CHOL 13mg; IRON 3.6mg; SODIUM 788mg; CALC 156mg

If your kids don't like eggplant, tuck several leaves of baby spinach into their wraps instead.

Sweet-Tart Kale Salad

Hands-on time: 8 min. Total time: 8 min.

Unlike most dressed salads, this one actually gets better with time. Though kale can be chewy, the lemony dressing softens the leaves the longer it's stashed in the fridge—but it still stays crunchy for a couple of days. If you chop your own kale, be sure to remove the stems.

¼ cup olive oil
3 tablespoons fresh lemon
  juice
¼ teaspoon salt
1 garlic clove, minced

6 cups loosely packed
  chopped kale
¼ cup chopped dried
  cherries
¼ cup chopped pecans

1. Combine first 4 ingredients in a large bowl, stirring well with a whisk. Add remaining ingredients, tossing to coat. Serve immediately, or cover and store in refrigerator up to 2 days.

SERVES 6 (serving size: 1 cup)

CALORIES 167; **FAT** 12.8g (1.6g sat, 8.5g mono, 2.2g poly); **PROTEIN** 3.0g; **CARB** 12.4g; **FIBER** 2.3g; **CHOL** 0mg; **IRON** 1.4mg; **SODIUM** 128 mg; **CALC** 98mg

Marbled Chocolate-Banana Bread

Hands-on time: 21 min. Total time: 1 hr. 50 min.

Having a loaf of this around means you'll have an easy dessert or even a sweet alternative to dinner rolls. You can also spread nut butter between thick slices for a portable meal or hearty snack after sports practice.

9 ounces all-purpose flour (about 2 cups)
3/4 teaspoon baking soda
1/2 teaspoon salt
1 cup sugar
1/4 cup butter, softened
1 1/2 cups mashed ripe banana (about 3 bananas)
1/2 cup egg substitute
1/3 cup plain low-fat yogurt
1/2 cup semisweet chocolate chips
Cooking spray

1. Preheat oven to 350°.

2. Weigh or lightly spoon flour into dry measuring cups; level with a knife. Combine flour, baking soda, and salt, stirring with a whisk.

3. Place sugar and butter in a large bowl; beat with a mixer at medium speed until well blended (about 1 minute). Add banana, egg substitute, and yogurt; beat until blended. Add flour mixture; beat at low speed just until moist.

4. Place chocolate chips in a medium microwave-safe bowl, and microwave at HIGH 1 minute or until almost melted, stirring until smooth. Cool slightly. Add 1 cup batter to chocolate, stirring until well combined. Spoon chocolate batter alternately with plain batter into an 8 1/2 x 4 1/2-inch loaf pan coated with cooking spray. Swirl batters together using a knife.

5. Bake at 350° for 1 hour and 15 minutes or until a wooden pick inserted in center comes out clean. Cool 10 minutes in pan on a wire rack; remove from pan. Cool completely on wire rack.

SERVES 16 (serving size: 1 slice)

CALORIES 183; **FAT** 4.7g (sat 2.8g, mono 1.4g, poly 0.2g); **PROTEIN** 3.1g; **CARB** 33.4g; **FIBER** 1.3g; **CHOL** 8mg; **IRON** 1.1mg; **SODIUM** 180mg; **CALC** 18mg

SMART STRATEGY

Make it official. Once you've scheduled a family dinner, send everyone an invite. It could be as simple as a note in a lunchbox, a text to a teen, or a notation on an online family calendar. Have fun with it. Mention what's on the menu and even a silly topic of conversation.

I'M ON A DIET, THEY'RE NOT

Healthy Foods Everyone Will Love

When my husband and I first started dating as 20-somethings, his dinners typically consisted of frozen chicken patties, **macaroni and cheese, or spaghetti**—or quite possibly all three on the same plate. Rest assured, there wasn't a green vegetable in sight. For a while, I went along for the ride. Until I realized how much I missed salad—and, more alarmingly, how snug my jeans were becoming.

Over the years, we've met in the middle: He eats the salads I make, and I honor his love for carbs by including some form of noodle, potato, or bread in the meal. But add two kids to the mix, and it can be hard to make everyone happy without straying from the way **I want to eat to feel good—and to fit into my jeans.**

TRY THIS!

Make the same meal for everyone.

If you're chopping onions, squeezing lemons, and skewering chicken for your family every night, don't you dare sit down to a low-calorie frozen dinner or diet shake in the name of weight loss! If there's one piece of advice I would include in almost every chapter it would be this:

Make one meal every night.
(Okay, most nights.)

Only one. For everyone. Why? Because it makes sense if you're pressed for time, if you have a picky eater, if your cupboards are bare, or if you're on a budget. It just makes sense. Being a short-order cook doesn't help you (hello, added work!) or your kids (they'll never learn to branch out if they're eating hot dogs every night for dinner).

Fact is, the foods that help you look and feel your best are the foods the rest of your family should be eating, too: fruits, vegetables, and lean proteins like chicken, fish, and beans. So instead of thinking about food as either "food that's good for health and weight loss" or "food my family likes," just think of it all as, well, food.

Modify your meal.

You're still cooking just one meal. (And for the record, microwaving a few chicken nuggets for your toddler counts as an additional meal.) You're just altering your plate. Though all the recipes in this book meet *Cooking Light*'s criteria—with healthy caps on calories, fat, and sodium—you can also do a couple more things to help meet your weight-loss goals.

• Add a large bowl of salad greens, a plate of sliced melon, or even just a bag of baby carrots to the spread. That way, you can take a smaller portion of the main course, and still have plenty of food to satisfy your appetite. And your unsuspecting spouse and kids will likely end up eating extra fruits and veggies, too (mwha-ha-ha!).

• Make some simple tweaks to your meal that don't involve cooking. Starchy carbs are often the easiest to cut back on when you're trying to lose weight. So use just one slice of bread on your sandwich to make it "open faced," use lettuce instead of tortillas for wraps, or serve your burger without a bun.

Get your spouse on board.

I've heard tale of spouses who protest loudly at the dinner table when new and nutritious items appear at mealtime.

Thankfully, my husband knows better than to badmouth broccoli. Plus, I always know when I've served something outside his comfort zone: He chews in a manner that silently communicates, "I am trying to chew this in a way that prevents me from actually tasting it."

The bottom line is that changes that help your health will help your family's health, too. So it's important that your spouse supports your decision. Otherwise, the habits won't stick, and your kids won't learn anything from it other than mom and dad like to fight about asparagus. That means no negative comments about what's on the table and no sabotaging by bringing out different foods.

Shrimp Tacos with Green Apple Salsa

Hands-on time: 35 min. Total time: 50 min.

Grilling the shrimp gives them a great look and flavor, but if you don't have a grill pan, use an outdoor grill or simply sauté them on the stove. To make a slaw instead of salsa, grate the apple instead of slicing it. Serve with mashed black beans.

1½ tablespoons olive oil, divided

4 teaspoons fresh lime juice, divided

¼ teaspoon ground cumin

¼ teaspoon hot smoked paprika

¼ teaspoon ground red pepper

1 pound medium shrimp, peeled and deveined

⅓ cup sliced green onions

¼ teaspoon salt, divided

½ teaspoon grated lime rind

1 Granny Smith apple, thinly sliced

1 minced seeded jalapeño pepper (optional)

8 (6-inch) corn tortillas

1 ounce crumbled queso fresco

Queso fresco is a soft Mexican cheese. Substitute feta cheese if you can't find it.

1. Combine 1 tablespoon olive oil, 2 teaspoons lime juice, cumin, paprika, and red pepper in a large zip-top plastic bag. Add shrimp to bag; seal bag, and toss to coat. Let stand 15 minutes.

2. Combine ½ tablespoon oil, 2 teaspoons juice, onions, ⅛ teaspoon salt, rind, apple, and, if desired, jalapeño; toss.

3. Remove shrimp from bag; discard marinade. Heat a grill pan over medium-high heat. Sprinkle shrimp with ⅛ teaspoon salt. Arrange half of shrimp in pan; grill 2 minutes on each side or until done. Remove from pan; keep warm. Repeat procedure with remaining shrimp. Toast tortillas in grill pan, if desired. Place 2 tortillas on each of 4 plates, and divide shrimp among tortillas. Divide salsa among tacos, and top evenly with queso fresco.

SERVES 4 (serving size: 2 tacos)

CALORIES 259; **FAT** 9.4g (sat 1.6g, mono 5.3g, poly 1.7g); **PROTEIN** 21.2g; **CARB** 24.3g; **FIBER** 3g; **CHOL** 170mg; **IRON** 3mg; **SODIUM** 364mg; **CALC** 87mg

Poached Halibut with Lemon-Herb Sauce

Hands-on time: 15 min. Total time: 25 min.

I confess: I'd never tried poaching fish until I made this recipe—but now I'm sold. Simmering the halibut in liquid is speedy and keeps it moist, which is good for folks like me who are prone to overcooking fish. Serve it with sautéed vegetables.

3 tablespoons olive oil
1½ tablespoons chopped seeded jalapeño pepper
1 tablespoon grated lemon rind
1½ tablespoons fresh lemon juice
4 teaspoons chopped fresh cilantro
4 teaspoons chopped fresh parsley
½ teaspoon salt
3 lemon sections, finely chopped
6 cups water
1 teaspoon salt
½ teaspoon black peppercorns
2 green onions, coarsely chopped
4 parsley sprigs
4 cilantro sprigs
4 (6-ounce) halibut fillets

1. Combine first 8 ingredients in a small bowl.

2. Combine 6 cups water and next 5 ingredients (through cilantro sprigs) in a large skillet; bring to a low simmer. Add fish; cook 10 minutes or until fish flakes easily when tested with a fork or until desired degree of doneness. Remove fish from pan with a slotted spoon; drain on paper towels. Serve with sauce.

SERVES 4 (serving size: 1 fillet and 1 tablespoon sauce)

CALORIES 217; **FAT** 11.2g (sat 1.6g, mono 7.5g, poly 1.4g); **PROTEIN** 27g; **CARB** 1.3g; **FIBER** 0.4g; **CHOL** 65mg; **IRON** 0.8mg; **SODIUM** 447mg; **CALC** 22mg

Halibut is an easy-to-find fish with a mild flavor, and it's also a sustainable choice.

Rosemary Oven-Fried Chicken

Hands-on time: 15 min. Total time: 40 min.

We were all wowed by this decadent-tasting dish with its nutty coating and drizzle of honey. For a less spicy coating, decrease the red pepper or just leave it out.

¼ cup nonfat buttermilk
2 tablespoons Dijon mustard
4 (4-ounce) chicken cutlets
⅓ cup whole-wheat panko
   (Japanese breadcrumbs)
⅓ cup finely chopped
   dry-roasted cashews
¾ teaspoon minced fresh
   rosemary

¼ teaspoon kosher salt
¼ teaspoon freshly ground
   black pepper
¼ teaspoon ground red
   pepper
Cooking spray
4 teaspoons honey

1. Preheat oven to 425°.

2. Combine buttermilk and mustard in a shallow dish, stirring with a whisk. Add chicken to buttermilk mixture, turning to coat.

3. Heat a small skillet over medium-high heat. Add panko to pan; cook 3 minutes or until golden, stirring frequently. Combine panko, cashews, and next 4 ingredients (through ground red pepper) in a shallow dish. Remove chicken from buttermilk mixture; dredge in panko mixture.

4. Arrange chicken on a wire rack coated with cooking spray in a foil-lined jelly-roll pan. Bake at 425° for 25 minutes or until chicken is done. Drizzle each cutlet with 1 teaspoon honey.

SERVES 4 (serving size: 1 cutlet)

CALORIES 248; FAT 8.7g (sat 1.8g, mono 4.2g, poly 1.4g); PROTEIN 27.4g; CARB 15.1g; FIBER 1.1g; CHOL 73mg; IRON 1.4mg; SODIUM 375mg; CALC 30mg

REAL MOM, REAL SMART

Measure, measure, measure. We all eat the same things, but I eat less of it. On spaghetti night, I measure out my portion of meat, sauce, and pasta before I mix it all together for the rest of the family. Sometimes it's a pain to measure everything, but it beats eating frozen "lite" meals while my family eats real food.

—Shandra Locken, Scottsdale, AZ

STOVETOP Maple-Mustard Glazed Chicken

Hands-on time: 20 min. Total time: 35 min.

On paper, chicken broth, maple syrup, mustard, garlic, and vinegar seems like an odd combo. But together they create the most deliciously sweet and tangy sauce. I'd strongly suggest serving this with rice to soak up every last bit. My husband's three-word review: "This. Is. Scrumptious."

2 teaspoons olive oil
4 (6-ounce) skinless, bone-less chicken breast halves
½ teaspoon freshly ground black pepper
¼ teaspoon salt
¼ cup fat-free, lower-sodium chicken broth

¼ cup maple syrup
2 teaspoons chopped fresh thyme
2 medium garlic cloves, thinly sliced
1 tablespoon cider vinegar
1 tablespoon stone-ground mustard

1. Preheat oven to 400°.

2. Heat a large ovenproof skillet over medium-high heat. Add oil to pan; swirl to coat. Sprinkle chicken with pepper and salt. Add chicken to pan; sauté 2 minutes on each side or until browned. Remove chicken from pan. Add broth, syrup, thyme, and garlic to pan; bring to a boil, scraping pan to loosen browned bits. Cook 2 minutes, stirring frequently. Add vinegar and mustard; cook 1 minute, stirring constantly. Return chicken to pan, and spoon mustard mixture over chicken. Bake at 400° for 10 minutes or until chicken is done. Remove chicken from pan; let stand 5 minutes. Place pan over medium heat; cook mustard mixture 2 minutes or until liquid is syrupy, stirring frequently. Serve with chicken.

SERVES 4 (serving size: 1 chicken breast half and 2 tablespoons sauce)

CALORIES 264; **FAT** 4.4g (sat 0.9g, mono 2.2g, poly 0.7g); **PROTEIN** 39.5g; **CARB** 14.2g; **FIBER** 0.2g; **CHOL** 99mg; **IRON** 1.6mg; **SODIUM** 337mg; **CALC** 38mg

CRAZY TRICK
that actually works!

Use your salad plate for your main course and your dinner plate for your salad. Research shows that we're satisfied with less food when it's served on smaller plates. Likewise, putting your salad on a larger plate will encourage you to pile on more veggies, which are filling thanks to a high fiber and water content.

Seared Tofu with Greens and Almond Dressing

Hands-on time: 35 min. Total time: 65 min.

The wasabi-flavored almonds add a touch of heat to this salad, but feel free to use regular almonds instead.

½ cup chopped wasabi and soy sauce–flavored almonds, divided (such as Blue Diamond)

5 tablespoons canola oil, divided

⅓ cup miso (soybean paste)

⅓ cup mirin (sweet rice wine)

⅓ cup rice vinegar

1 tablespoon refrigerated ginger paste (such as Gourmet Garden)

2 (14-ounce) packages water-packed firm tofu, drained

4 cups gourmet salad greens

4 cups shredded napa (Chinese) cabbage

2 cups shredded carrot (about 2 large)

1 cup fresh cilantro leaves

1. Combine ¼ cup almonds, 3 tablespoons oil, and next 4 ingredients (through ginger paste) in a small bowl, stirring well with a whisk.

2. Cut each tofu block crosswise into 9 slices. Place tofu slices on several layers of paper towels; cover with additional paper towels. Place a large heavy skillet over tofu slices. Let stand 30 minutes. Discard paper towels.

3. Heat a large nonstick skillet over medium-high heat. Add 1 tablespoon oil to pan; swirl to coat. Add 9 tofu slices to pan; cook 4 minutes on each side or until browned. Remove from pan; drain on paper towels. Repeat procedure with 1 tablespoon oil and tofu slices.

4. Combine salad greens, cabbage, carrot, and cilantro in a large bowl; toss gently. Place 2 cups salad on each of 6 plates. Top each salad with 3 tofu slices and 3 tablespoons miso dressing. Sprinkle with remaining ¼ cup chopped almonds.

SERVES 6 (serving size: 1 salad)

CALORIES 315; **FAT** 22.3g (sat 2.1g, mono 7.6g, poly 3.9g); **PROTEIN** 12g; **CARB** 17.8g; **FIBER** 5.5g; **CHOL** 0mg; **IRON** 2.7mg; **SODIUM** 665mg; **CALC** 133mg

SMART STRATEGY

Never say "diet." No matter how aggravated you are about your I've-had-two-kids belly, avoid talking about dieting or your weight in front of your kids—because negative attitudes about food and your body are contagious. Research has shown that kids (especially girls) are more likely to be preoccupied about their weight if their moms are frequent dieters. If you want your kids to have a healthy relationship with food and a good body image, model those behaviors for them.

Black Bean Taco Salad with Lime Vinaigrette

Hands-on time: 15 min. Total time: 15 min.

With lots of fiber and protein, this Southwestern-inspired salad—dressed in a light vinaigrette—is satisfying even if you skip the chips for your portion.

Vinaigrette:
1/4 cup chopped seeded tomato
1/4 cup chopped fresh cilantro
2 tablespoons olive oil
1 tablespoon cider vinegar
1 teaspoon grated lime rind
1 tablespoon fresh lime juice
1/4 teaspoon salt
1/4 teaspoon ground cumin
1/4 teaspoon chili powder
1/4 teaspoon black pepper
1 garlic clove, peeled

Salad:
8 cups thinly sliced iceberg lettuce
1 1/2 cups chopped cooked chicken breast
1 cup chopped tomato
1 cup chopped green bell pepper
1 cup finely diced red onion
2 ounces reduced-fat shredded sharp cheddar cheese (about 1/2 cup)
1 (15-ounce) can black beans, rinsed and drained
4 cups fat-free baked tortilla chips (about 4 ounces)

Rinsing canned beans helps remove some of the sodium.

1. To prepare vinaigrette, place first 11 ingredients in a blender or food processor; process until smooth.

2. To prepare salad, combine lettuce and next 6 ingredients (through black beans) in a large bowl. Add vinaigrette; toss well to coat. Serve immediately with chips.

Note: To make ahead, combine all salad ingredients, except iceberg lettuce, with vinaigrette in a large bowl; cover and refrigerate up to 2 days. Just before serving, add iceberg lettuce, and toss to coat. Serve with chips.

SERVES 4 (serving size: about 2 cups salad and 1 cup chips)

CALORIES 402; **FAT** 12.6g (sat 3.2g, mono 6.5g, poly 1.9g); **PROTEIN** 24.5g; **CARB** 51.6g; **FIBER** 8g; **CHOL** 35mg; **IRON** 3.6mg; **SODIUM** 861mg; **CALC** 236mg

Asian-Style Veggie Rolls

Hands-on time: 30 min. Total time: 30 min.

When the dipping sauce is made first, it has just enough time for the flavors to meld. For the assembly of the rolls, have your kids join in. They are much more likely to eat them if they participate in the prep.

Sauce:
1 tablespoon sugar
3 tablespoons fresh lime
   juice (about 1 lime)
3 tablespoons water
2 tablespoons fish sauce
1 garlic clove, minced
1 Thai chile, thinly sliced
   (optional)
Rolls:
8 (8-inch) round sheets rice
   paper

2 cups thinly sliced Bibb
   lettuce leaves (about
   4 large)
2 cups cooked bean threads
   (cellophane noodles)
1 cup fresh bean sprouts
1 cup shredded carrot
1/2 cup coarsely chopped
   fresh mint
1/2 cup fresh cilantro leaves
1/4 cup thinly sliced green
   onions

You'll find rice paper and cellophane noodles in the ethnic foods aisle of the grocery store.

1. To prepare sauce, combine sugar, next 4 ingredients (through garlic), and, if desired, Thai chile in a small bowl, stirring with a whisk until sugar dissolves.

2. To prepare rolls, add hot water to a large, shallow dish to a depth of 1 inch. Place 1 rice paper sheet in dish, and let stand 30 seconds or just until soft. Place sheet on a flat surface. Arrange 1/4 cup lettuce over half of sheet, leaving a 1/2-inch border. Top with 1/4 cup bean threads, 2 tablespoons sprouts, 2 tablespoons carrot, 1 tablespoon mint, 1 tablespoon cilantro leaves, and 11/2 teaspoons green onions. Folding sides of sheet over filling and starting with filled side, roll up jelly-roll fashion. Gently press seam to seal. Place roll, seam side down, on a serving platter and cover. Repeat procedure with remaining roll ingredients, covering rolls after each addition to keep from drying. Serve rolls with dipping sauce.

SERVES 8 (serving size: 1 roll and about 2 teaspoons sauce)

CALORIES 83; **FAT** 0.3g (sat 0g, mono 0g, poly 0.1g); **PROTEIN** 2.3g; **CARB** 18.5g; **FIBER** 1.1g; **CHOL** 0mg; **IRON** 0.7mg; **SODIUM** 371mg; **CALC** 22mg

DINNERTIME SURVIVAL GUIDE

TOP 5 TIPS FOR RAISING HEALTHY EATERS

#1

NIX "GOOD" AND "BAD" FOODS. Cookies aren't "bad," and you're not "good" because you ate a salad. These unhelpful labels are especially confusing for kids.

#2

AVOID FOOD REWARDS. They work in the moment, but they can also create a pattern of emotional eating that won't serve your child well in the long run. (Tough day at work? Ice cream!)

#3

RESPECT THEIR APPETITES. Keep regular meal and snack times, and always let your kids stop eating when they say they're full (just save leftovers for later).

#4

MAKE IT EASY. Healthy choices are simple to make if you have fruit on the counter and cut up veggies within easy reach—and junk food kept to a minimum.

#5

GIVE SOME FREEDOM. Hovering over your kids' every choice won't teach them to navigate food in the real world. Communicate your food values, and then let them practice on their own. They won't always get it "right," and that's okay.

Butternut Squash Soup

Hands-on time: 25 min. Total time: 50 min.

Granny Smith apple gives this sweet, creamy soup a hit of tartness. If you want to kick up the flavor a notch, add a dash of hot sauce to each serving.

1 tablespoon butter
3½ cups cubed peeled butternut squash (about 1¼ pounds)
1 cup chopped peeled Granny Smith apple
½ cup chopped Vidalia or other sweet onion

3½ cups organic vegetable broth
¼ cup half-and-half
⅛ teaspoon salt
Cracked black pepper, reduced-fat sour cream, fresh thyme sprigs (optional)

1. Melt butter in a large saucepan over medium-high heat. Add squash, apple, and onion; sauté 8 minutes. Add broth, and bring to a boil. Cover, reduce heat, and simmer 25 minutes or until squash is tender. Remove from heat; stir in half-and-half and salt.

2. Place half of squash mixture in a blender. Remove center piece of blender lid (to allow steam to escape); secure blender lid on blender. Place a clean towel over opening in blender lid (to avoid splatters). Blend until smooth. Pour into saucepan. Repeat procedure with remaining squash mixture. Garnish with cracked black pepper, sour cream, and thyme sprigs, if desired.

SERVES 6 (serving size: about 1 cup)

CALORIES 98; **FAT** 3.5g (sat 2g, mono 0.8g, poly 0.2g); **PROTEIN** 1.9g; **CARB** 16.5g; **FIBER** 2.7g; **CHOL** 8mg; **IRON** 0.8mg; **SODIUM** 342mg; **CALC** 66mg

Other sweet onions include Walla Walla and Imperial.

SMART STRATEGY

Keep low-calorie soups like this one on hand as a first course. Research from Penn State University found that people ate 20 percent less at lunch when they started their meal with soup because it's so filling.

Lemony Chicken Soup with Rice

Hands-on time: 20 min. Total time: 36 min.

My husband orders a similar soup, called avgolemono, whenever we're at a Greek restaurant, but he raves about this kid-friendly Cooking Light *version, too.*

2 teaspoons olive oil
1/2 cup chopped onion
3 garlic cloves, minced
6 1/2 cups fat-free, lower-sodium chicken broth
1/2 cup uncooked long-grain rice
1/3 cup fresh lemon juice
2 teaspoons cornstarch
1/2 teaspoon salt
1/2 teaspoon freshly ground black pepper
1 large egg, lightly beaten
2 cups shredded cooked chicken breast
2 tablespoons chopped fresh parsley
2 tablespoons torn fresh basil

1. Heat a Dutch oven over medium-high heat. Add oil to pan; swirl to coat. Add onion and garlic; sauté 2 minutes. Add broth; bring to a boil. Stir in rice; reduce heat, and simmer 16 minutes.

2. Combine juice, cornstarch, salt, pepper, and egg in a small bowl, stirring with a whisk. Slowly pour egg into broth mixture, stirring constantly with a whisk. Add chicken to broth mixture; cook until mixture thickens and rice is done, stirring occasionally. Top with parsley and basil.

SERVES 4 (serving size: 1 1/2 cups)

CALORIES 269; FAT 7g (sat 1.5g, mono 3.5g, poly 1.1g); PROTEIN 25.4g; CARB 25.7g; FIBER 1.1g; CHOL 116mg; IRON 2.1mg; SODIUM 541mg; CALC 54mg

SPEEDY Spinach Dip

Hands-on time: 8 min. Total time: 38 min.

This normally high-damage dip gets a makeover with Greek yogurt and reduced-fat cream cheese. Serve it with toasted baguette slices, baked pita chips, and fresh vegetables.

¾ cup plain fat-free Greek yogurt

3 ounces crumbled feta cheese (about ¾ cup)

2 ounces ⅓-less-fat cream cheese, softened (about ¼ cup)

¼ cup reduced-fat sour cream

1 garlic clove, crushed

1½ cups finely chopped fresh spinach

1 tablespoon fresh dill

⅛ teaspoon freshly ground black pepper

1. Place yogurt, feta cheese, cream cheese, sour cream, and crushed garlic in a food processor; process until smooth.

2. Spoon yogurt mixture into a medium bowl; stir in spinach, dill, and black pepper. Cover and chill at least 30 minutes.

SERVES 8 (serving size: ¼ cup)

CALORIES 79; **FAT** 5.5g (sat 3.5g, mono 1.3g, poly 0.2g); **PROTEIN** 5g; **CARB** 2.6g; **FIBER** 0.1g; **CHOL** 20mg; **IRON** 0.3mg; **SODIUM** 199mg; **CALC** 109mg

CRAZY TRICK
that actually works!

Are you a scavenger—grabbing up abandoned pizza crusts and finishing what's left behind on your kids' plates? I once asked a client to put all those little bites in a bowl on the counter each day instead of eating them. Not only was she disgusted by the sad pile of half-eaten apples and Goldfish crackers, but she ended up losing 10 pounds.

Sugar Snap Peas with Zesty Lemon Dressing

Hands-on time: 18 min. Total time: 18 min.

Taking a few extra steps to make veggies look and taste even better encourages you (and your kids) to eat more of them. If your kids like snap peas better raw, you can still toss them in the dressing.

8 cups water
12 ounces sugar snap peas, trimmed
1/2 teaspoon grated lemon rind
2 tablespoons fresh lemon juice
1 tablespoon extra-virgin olive oil
1 teaspoon Dijon mustard
1/2 teaspoon sugar
1/4 teaspoon kosher salt
1/4 teaspoon black pepper
1 shallot, minced

1. Bring 8 cups water to a boil in a large Dutch oven. Add peas; cook 30 seconds or until crisp-tender. Drain and plunge into ice water; drain. Slice half of peas diagonally.

2. Combine lemon rind and remaining ingredients in a medium bowl; stir with a whisk. Add peas; toss to coat.

SERVES 4 (serving size: 1 cup)

CALORIES 73; **FAT** 3.6g (sat 0.5g, mono 2.5g, poly 0.4g); **PROTEIN** 2.5g; **CARB** 8.4g; **FIBER** 2.3g; **CHOL** 0mg; **IRON** 1.8mg; **SODIUM** 154mg; **CALC** 39mg

MAKE-AHEAD Chocolate-Date-Nut Squares

Hands-on time: 15 min. Total time: 45 min.

Adapted from a recipe by dietitian Danielle Omar of foodconfidence.com, these snacks are packed with filling dried fruit and nuts so I'm satisfied with just one—but still feel like I got my chocolate fix.

Cooking spray
2 cups dried dates
1 cup sunflower seed kernels
1 cup walnut halves
1/2 cup sliced almonds
1/4 cup unsweetened cocoa

1/4 cup semisweet chocolate morsels
1/4 cup flaked unsweetened coconut
1/4 cup fat-free milk

1. Line bottom and sides of an 8-inch square metal baking pan with foil, allowing 2 to 3 inches to extend over sides; lightly coat foil with cooking spray.

2. Place dates in a food processor; process until chopped. Add sunflower seed kernels and next 5 ingredients (through coconut); process until nuts are chopped.

3. Drizzle with milk; process until well blended, stopping to scrape down sides. Press mixture into prepared pan. Freeze 30 minutes; cut into squares.

SERVES 16 (serving size: 1 square)

CALORIES 191; **FAT** 11.4g (sat 2.5g, mono 2.5g, poly 6g); **PROTEIN** 4.3g; **CARB** 22.5g; **FIBER** 4g; **CHOL** 0mg; **IRON** 1.1mg; **SODIUM** 3mg; **CALC** 37mg

REAL MOM, REAL SMART

I don't deprive myself. All four of us have a sweet tooth, so we have something sweet once a day, like a piece of dark chocolate or some ice cream. It works because we eat mindfully, so we feel satisfied.

—Maryann Jacobsen, RD, blogger, rasiehealthyeaters.com

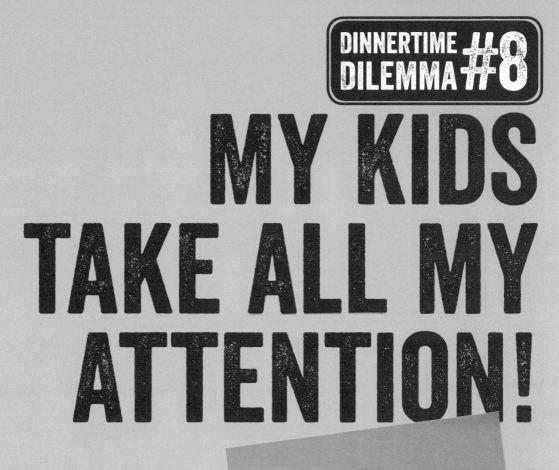

MY KIDS TAKE ALL MY ATTENTION!

One-Handed Recipes—Almost

Before we had kids, my husband and I would leisurely cook meals together, talking in great detail about our respective days as if we had all the time in the world (because we did). Then we'd take our steaming plates of food to the couch, and watch TV. Did I mention all of this took place at 8 p.m.?

Two kids later, dinner prep looks a lot different. For starters, it's happening three hours earlier when only one of us (lucky me!) is home. And there's nothing leisurely about it. There were many nights I had a baby perched on my hip while trying to cook. Eventually I started making something I called Mommy's Famous One-Handed Spaghetti, which was just whole-wheat spaghetti and bottled sauce with some garlic thrown in. **Because who has time to simmer homemade marinara all day when you have two small kids?**

Keep your kids busy.

When I was growing up, moms who were cooking dinner sent their kids outside and warned them not to come back until they were called. I'm pretty sure that's considered child endangerment by today's standards, so here are a few other ideas for keeping your offspring out of your hair.

Strategic screen time: I know screens should never be a babysitter (and kids younger than two aren't even supposed to be tuning in). But a friend of mine once gave me this piece of wisdom: Dole out screen time when it's most helpful to you. Are my boys losing brain cells with every episode of *Phineas and Ferb*? Not likely, but it's a risk I'm willing to take for 30 to 45 minutes of peace to cook dinner every night.

Audio books: I'm amazed by the trance-like state that comes over my children when they listen to a book on CD. Borrow a few from the library or download them on the Internet from sites like Amazon and Audible.

Dinnertime fun box: This is a great plan for younger ones. Pack a little box of toys, crafts, and games that are only available while you're cooking dinner. Try assembling a few dinnertime fun boxes, and rotate them as needed.

Chores: If your kids have daily chores, schedule them for the pre-dinner hour (just make sure it's nothing that requires your help).

Enlist helpers.

I get it: Cooking with kids can slow you down and test your patience. But for those nights when you can swing it, a little child labor may be just what you need to keep them occupied and you productive.

Toddlers & preschoolers can:
- ❑ Put place mats and napkins on the table
- ❑ Snap the ends off green beans
- ❑ Put liners in a muffin tin
- ❑ Sprinkle nuts on a salad
- ❑ Tear lettuce
- ❑ Shuck corn
- ❑ Stir batter

School-age children can:
- ❑ Pour drinks and set out plates and silverware
- ❑ Operate a food processor or hand mixer
- ❑ Peel potatoes and mash them
- ❑ Cut herbs with kitchen scissors
- ❑ Squeeze garlic through a press
- ❑ Measure liquid ingredients
- ❑ Grate cheese

(Continued)

TAKE SOME SHORTCUTS IN THE KITCHEN.

When the troops are restless and hungry, every second counts. Here are some timesavers that make meal prep faster:

TIME SAVED	KITCHEN SHORTCUT
5 minutes	Use bags of prewashed, preprepped vegetables such as broccoli slaw and cauliflower florets.
40 minutes	Cook baked potatoes in the microwave instead of the oven.
2 minutes	Set out your non-perishable dinner ingredients in the morning.
1.5 or 2 hours	Use a store-bought rotisserie chicken instead of roasting your own.
2 minutes	Use bottled minced garlic instead of taking the time to peel and mince fresh garlic.
35 minutes	Microwave a packet of precooked whole-grain brown rice instead of making it on the stove.
3 minutes	Chop vegetables or nuts in a mini chopper or food processor instead of by hand.
6 minutes	Mix components of the meal—like casserole toppings, sauces, or marinades—in the morning, and refrigerate them.

Sweet and Spicy Citrus Tilapia

Hands-on time: 23 min. Total time: 38 min.

This superfast fish was a big hit with my kids—and a 9-year-old dinner guest even proclaimed it was the best fish he'd ever had. I left out the red pepper that evening, and let those who wanted a touch of heat sprinkle a little on their serving once the fish was done. I served it with whole-wheat egg noodles and asparagus.

4 (6-ounce) tilapia fillets
Cooking spray
1/2 cup fresh orange juice (about 1 orange)
3 tablespoons fresh lime juice (about 1 1/2 limes)
1 tablespoon brown sugar
1 tablespoon extra-virgin olive oil

2 teaspoons lower-sodium soy sauce
1/2 teaspoon salt
1/2 teaspoon ground cumin
1/4 teaspoon black pepper
1/4 teaspoon ground red pepper
2 garlic cloves, crushed
1/2 teaspoon paprika

1. Arrange fish in a single layer in a shallow roasting pan coated with cooking spray. Combine orange juice and next 9 ingredients (through garlic); pour over fish. Let stand 15 minutes.

2. Preheat broiler.

3. Sprinkle fish with paprika; broil 12 minutes or until fish flakes easily when tested with a fork or until desired degree of doneness. Drizzle sauce over fish.

If you don't have a roasting pan, use an ovenproof skillet.

SERVES 4 (serving size: 1 fillet and about 2 teaspoons sauce)

CALORIES 225; **FAT** 6.6g (sat 1.5g, mono 3.4g, poly 1.2g); **PROTEIN** 34.8g; **CARB** 7.5g; **FIBER** 0.4g; **CHOL** 85mg; **IRON** 1.3mg; **SODIUM** 486mg; **CALC** 30mg

Hands-on time: 15 min. Total time: 30 min.

Place squares of foil on the countertop, and set up an assembly line with veggies so everyone can add their own. Top each square with a salmon fillet, seal, and bake. Let the kids peer through the oven window toward the end of the baking time to see the packets puff up. When time's up, you can either remove the baked fish and veggies from the packets to plates or let everyone eat right from the foil.

1³/₄ cups sliced zucchini	2 tablespoons butter, cut
1 cup red bell pepper strips	into 4 equal pieces
8 lemon slices	4 dill sprigs
4 (6-ounce) skinless salmon	½ teaspoon kosher salt
fillets	½ teaspoon black pepper

1. Preheat oven to 400°.

2. Cut 4 (14-inch) squares of foil. Place zucchini, red bell pepper, and lemon slices in center of foil squares. Top each with a salmon fillet, butter, and dill sprig; sprinkle with salt and pepper. Fold foil over fish and vegetables; tightly seal edges.

3. Place foil packets on a jelly-roll pan. Bake at 400° for 15 to 20 minutes or until fish flakes easily when tested with a fork or until desired degree of doneness. Remove from oven; cut open packets and serve.

SERVES 4 (serving size: 1 packet)

CALORIES 345; **FAT** 18.3g (sat 5.6g, mono 5.6g, poly 5.2g); **PROTEIN** 39.5g; **CARB** 3.7g; **FIBER** 1g; **CHOL** 123mg; **IRON** 1.9mg; **SODIUM** 381mg; **CALC** 38mg

---

SMART STRATEGY

Kid-proof the kitchen with these safety precautions:

- *Turn saucepan handles toward the back of the stove.*
- *Keep food processors, blenders, and other small appliances unplugged if your child can reach them.*
- *Use plastic measuring cups instead of glass.*
- *Make sure kids know that electric and ceramic glass stovetops may still be hot even when burners are off.*
- *Always supervise kids who are using knives, and have them keep the blade pointed away from them.*

Cheeseburger Pasta Bake

Hands-on time: 35 min. Total time: 1 hr. 30 min.

1 pound ground round
½ pound lean ground sausage
1 cup chopped onion
3 garlic cloves, crushed
4 tablespoons sun-dried tomato paste
1 tablespoon balsamic vinegar
1 teaspoon sugar
1 teaspoon dried thyme
1 teaspoon dried oregano
¼ teaspoon black pepper
1 (28-ounce) can whole tomatoes, undrained and chopped
1.5 ounces all-purpose flour (about ⅓ cup)
2½ cups 2% low-fat milk
4 ounces American cheese, cut into cubes
3 ounces shredded part-skim mozzarella cheese (about ¾ cup)
8 cups hot cooked penne
Shredded lettuce, red onion slices, diced tomatoes (optional)

1. Combine first 4 ingredients in a large nonstick skillet; cook over medium-high heat until browned, stirring to crumble. Add tomato paste and next 6 ingredients; stir well. Bring to a boil; reduce heat, and simmer, uncovered, 25 minutes, stirring occasionally. Set aside.

2. Preheat oven to 350°.

3. Weigh or lightly spoon flour into a dry measuring cup; level with a knife. Place flour in a saucepan. Gradually add milk, stirring with a whisk until blended. Cook over medium heat 10 minutes or until thick, stirring constantly. Stir in cheeses; cook 1 minute or until cheeses melt, stirring constantly. Reserve ½ cup cheese sauce. Pour remaining cheese sauce, beef mixture, and pasta into a 13 x 9-inch glass or ceramic baking dish, and stir gently. Drizzle with reserved cheese sauce.

4. Bake at 350° for 30 minutes or until thoroughly heated; top with lettuce, onion slices, and diced tomatoes, if desired.

SERVES 8 (serving size: ⅛ of casserole)

CALORIES 404; **FAT** 19g (sat 8.7g, mono 5.6g, poly 1g); **PROTEIN** 26.9g; **CARB** 30.8g; **FIBER** 2.3g; **CHOL** 84mg; **IRON** 3.5mg; **SODIUM** 592mg; **CALC** 308mg

SPEEDY Meat Loaf

Hands-on time: 12 min. Total time: 39 min.

It's a miracle: A meat loaf that bakes in less than 30 minutes. Rejoice! Then eat.

1 pound ground sirloin
⅓ cup chopped green onions
3 tablespoons dry breadcrumbs
2 teaspoons minced fresh garlic
½ teaspoon dry mustard
¼ teaspoon freshly ground black pepper
¼ teaspoon crushed red pepper
⅛ teaspoon salt
1 large egg, lightly beaten
6 tablespoons ketchup, divided
Cooking spray

1. Preheat oven to 400°.

2. Combine first 9 ingredients in a large bowl; add ¼ cup ketchup. Mix beef mixture with hands just until combined. Shape beef mixture into a 9 x 4–inch loaf on a broiler pan coated with cooking spray. Bake at 400° for 20 minutes. Brush top of meat loaf with 2 tablespoons ketchup. Bake an additional 7 minutes or until done. Cut loaf into 8 equal slices.

SERVES 4 (serving size: 2 slices)

CALORIES 267; **FAT** 13.1g (sat 5.1g, mono 5.5g, poly 0.7g); **PROTEIN** 25.6g; **CARB** 10.8g; **FIBER** 0.7g; **CHOL** 127mg; **IRON** 3.4mg; **SODIUM** 457mg; **CALC** 44mg

SMART STRATEGY

Do a speedy defrost. If you forgot to defrost the meat or poultry for dinner (story of my life), don't ditch your plan. Follow the USDA's advice: Seal your meat in a zip-top plastic bag, and submerge it in a bowl of cold water on the counter or in the sink, changing the water every 30 minutes. One-pound packages of meat and chicken should defrost within an hour. Or defrost it in the micro-wave, and then be sure to cook it immediately to pre-vent bacteria from growing.

DINNERTIME SURVIVAL GUIDE TOP 5

ISSUES NOT TO STRESS OVER

#1

EATING IN FRONT OF THE TV: It's a rare event (and should stay that way) but on a particularly crazy night when I let my kids do it, they act like they've won the lottery.

#2

AN OCCASIONAL SOFT DRINK: We don't keep sweet drinks in the house, so a soda or lemonade when we're out to eat or at a party doesn't faze me.

#3

FROZEN FOOD: Yes, I prefer making fresh, from-scratch meals. But sometimes dinner comes out of a box that was in the freezer. And that's okay.

#4

PAPER PLATES: My apologies to the planet, but when I've got a gaggle of kids over for pizza, a stack of paper plates is a time (and sanity) saver.

#5

KETCHUP.

"Roasted" Slow-Cooker Chicken

Hands-on time: 23 min. Total time: 4 hr. 23 min.

This chicken looks and tastes like you've been minding the oven for hours—when really, you just pushed a button. What could be better?

1 (3½-pound) whole chicken
4 teaspoons minced fresh
 rosemary, divided
3 tablespoons olive oil
1 teaspoon onion powder
1 teaspoon black pepper
¾ teaspoon salt

4 garlic cloves, minced
½ cup fat-free, lower-
 sodium chicken broth
2 tablespoons butter
1 tablespoon all-purpose
 flour
⅛ teaspoon black pepper

1. Remove and discard giblets and neck from chicken. Trim excess fat. Starting at neck cavity, loosen skin from breast by inserting fingers, gently pushing between skin and meat.

2. Combine 3 teaspoons rosemary, oil, and next 4 ingredients (through garlic). Rub seasoning mixture under loosened skin.

3. Pour broth into an electric slow cooker. Crumble 3 sheets of foil into small balls; place in bottom of slow cooker. Place chicken on top of foil balls.

4. Cover and cook on LOW for 4 hours. Place chicken on a platter, reserving drippings.

5. Melt butter in a small saucepan over medium heat. Add flour, stirring with a whisk until well blended. Cook 1 minute, stirring constantly. Add drippings from slow cooker; cook 2 minutes, stirring constantly. Remove from heat; stir in 1 teaspoon rosemary and ⅛ teaspoon black pepper.

SERVES 6 (serving size: 3 ounces chicken and about 2½ tablespoons gravy)

CALORIES 310; **FAT** 15.1g (sat 4.6g, mono 7.5g, poly 1.8g); **PROTEIN** 39.1g; **CARB** 2g; **FIBER** 0.3g; **CHOL** 115mg; **IRON** 1.5mg; **SODIUM** 465mg; **CALC** 29mg

CRAZY TRICK
that actually works!

If you want to cross the chicken's legs and tie them up before the chicken is "slow-cooker roasted," use cotton kitchen twine. If you find yourself without cooking twine, use plain dental floss as an alternative. It works great.

Chicken Tostadas

Hands-on time: 24 min. Total time: 43 min.

Treat your family to a new take on taco night. Instead of deep-frying the tortillas, you bake them until they're crisp. Pile up the tortillas, place all the toppings in little bowls, and let everyone make their own.

1 teaspoon garlic powder
1/2 teaspoon onion powder
1/4 teaspoon salt
1/4 teaspoon ground cumin
4 (6-ounce) skinless, boneless chicken breast halves
1 1/2 teaspoons olive oil
8 (6-inch) corn tortillas
Cooking spray

1/2 cup diced peeled mango
1/2 cup diced peeled avocado
3/4 cup refrigerated prepared pico de gallo
4 ounces preshredded reduced-fat 4-cheese Mexican-blend cheese (about 1 cup)
Lime wedges and cilantro sprigs (optional)

Pico de gallo is a fresh salsa found in the refrigerated section of the grocery store.

1. Preheat oven to 400°.

2. Combine first 4 ingredients; rub over chicken.

3. Heat a large nonstick skillet over medium-high heat. Add oil to pan; swirl to coat. Add chicken; cook 7 minutes on each side or until done. Remove chicken from pan; let stand 5 minutes. Cut into 1/4-inch-thick slices.

4. Coat both sides of tortillas with cooking spray. Place on a baking sheet, and bake at 400° for 7 to 8 minutes on each side or until lightly browned and crisp.

5. Divide chicken among baked tortillas; top each with 1 tablespoon mango, 1 tablespoon avocado, 1 1/2 tablespoons pico de gallo, and 2 tablespoons cheese. Garnish with lime wedges and cilantro sprigs, if desired.

SERVES 4 (serving size: 2 tostada stacks)

CALORIES 462; **FAT** 16g (sat 5.4g, mono 4.7g, poly 1.9g); **PROTEIN** 46.7g; **CARB** 31g; **FIBER** 4.9g; **CHOL** 124mg; **IRON** 1.5mg; **SODIUM** 732mg; **CALC** 460mg

Cider-Glazed Chicken with Browned Butter– Pecan Rice

Hands-on time: 26 min. Total time: 26 min.

This dish sounds elaborate but takes less than 30 minutes to prepare from start to finish. The sweet sauce on the chicken and the nutty rice make a great flavor combo. Serve with a side of steamed green beans.

1 (3.5-ounce) bag boil-in-bag brown rice (such as Uncle Ben's)

2 tablespoons butter, divided

1 pound chicken cutlets (about 4 cutlets)

¾ teaspoon salt, divided

¼ teaspoon freshly ground black pepper

½ cup refrigerated apple cider

1 teaspoon Dijon mustard

¼ cup chopped pecans

2 tablespoons chopped fresh flat-leaf parsley

1. Cook rice according to package directions, omitting salt and fat; drain.

2. While rice cooks, melt 1 teaspoon butter in a large heavy skillet over medium-high heat. Sprinkle chicken with ¼ teaspoon salt and pepper. Add chicken to pan; cook 3 minutes on each side or until done. Remove from pan. Add cider and mustard to pan, scraping pan to loosen browned bits; cook 2 to 3 minutes or until syrupy. Add chicken to pan, turning to coat. Remove from heat; set aside.

3. Melt 5 teaspoons butter in a saucepan over medium-high heat; cook 2 minutes or until browned and fragrant. Reduce heat to medium; add pecans, and cook 1 minute or until toasted, stirring frequently. Add parsley, rice and ½ teaspoon salt; toss well to coat. Serve rice with chicken.

SERVES 4 (serving size: 1 cutlet and ½ cup rice)

CALORIES 333; **FAT** 13g (sat 4.4g, mono 4.9g, poly 2.2g); **PROTEIN** 29.1g; **CARB** 24.2g; **FIBER** 1.9g; **CHOL** 81mg; **IRON** 1.5mg; **SODIUM** 601mg; **CALC** 23mg

CRAZY TRICK
that actually works!

Just for fun, sacrifice a bag or two of uncooked rice for your kids to play with while you're cooking. It's a great play material—especially for the littlest ones—because it fuels their sensory skills. Just dump it into a small tub, and add some measuring cups and scoops or pour it into a rimmed baking sheet, and add Matchbox-size cars and trucks. When they're done playing, pour the rice into a container labeled "play rice," and use it again and again.

Popeye's Baked Ziti

Hands-on time: 35 min. Total time: 1 hr. 3 min.

1½ cups 2% reduced-fat milk
1¼ cups finely chopped onion, divided
¼ teaspoon sea salt
3 (2-inch) thyme sprigs
1 bay leaf
1 tablespoon all-purpose flour
1 teaspoon olive oil
3 cups sliced mushrooms
1 cup chopped red bell pepper
1 (6-ounce) bag baby spinach
1 tablespoon chopped thyme

¼ teaspoon black pepper
1⅓ cups 2% low-fat cottage cheese
4 cups hot cooked ziti (about 6 ounces uncooked pasta)
2 cups shredded cooked chicken breast
4 ounces reduced-fat shredded sharp cheddar cheese (about 1 cup), divided
2 ounces grated fresh Parmesan cheese (about ½ cup), divided
Cooking spray

1. Combine milk, ¼ cup onion, salt, thyme, and bay leaf in a saucepan; bring to a boil. Remove from heat; cover and let stand 3 minutes.

2. Place flour in a small bowl. Add milk mixture; stir with a whisk until smooth. Return mixture to saucepan. Bring to a boil; cook 1 minute or until barely thick. Strain through a sieve over a bowl; discard solids.

3. Preheat oven to 375°. Heat a large nonstick skillet over medium-high heat. Add oil to pan; swirl to coat. Add mushrooms, 1 cup onion, and bell pepper; sauté 4 minutes or until tender. Add spinach, thyme, and black pepper; sauté 2 minutes or just until spinach wilts (mixture will be very moist).

4. Place cottage cheese in a food processor; process until very smooth. Combine spinach mixture, cottage cheese, pasta, chicken, ¾ cup cheddar cheese, ¼ cup Parmesan cheese, and sauce in a large bowl, stirring well. Spoon mixture into a 2-quart baking dish coated with cooking spray. Sprinkle with ¼ cup cheddar cheese and ¼ cup Parmesan cheese. Bake at 375° for 25 minutes or until bubbly.

SERVES 6 (serving size: ⅙ of casserole)

CALORIES 403; **FAT** 12g (sat 5.9g, mono 3.7g, poly 0.9g); **PROTEIN** 37.6g; **CARB** 36.6g; **FIBER** 3.8g; **CHOL** 68mg; **IRON** 3mg; **SODIUM** 654mg; **CALC** 439mg

---

If your kids are mushroom-phobic, finely chop them.

SMART STRATEGY

Make a pre-dinner snack. In that "witching hour" when you're cooking dinner and your kids are intermittently whining about being hungry and poking each other for no good reason, put some crudités or some of the vegetable you're making for dinner on a platter, and circulate it around. Or station it on the counter where kids can get to it. It's a good distraction for them—and if they don't touch veggies at dinnertime, you'll know they got some nibbles in already. If they eat even more, that's just icing on the (carrot) cake.

Italian Sausage Hoagies

Hands-on time: 31 min. Total time: 31 min.

Are these hoagies or subs? Depends where you live. Either way, they're a fun and fast spin on the classic meatball sub. Or hoagie. You get the idea. Hollowing out the bottom half of the rolls helps hold the sausage in place—a great help for little hands.

4 (2-ounce) hoagie rolls
9 ounces sweet turkey
  Italian sausage, cut into
  1-inch-thick pieces
½ cup prechopped onion
1 teaspoon minced fresh
  garlic
1 cup jarred organic pasta
  sauce (such as Amy's)

¼ teaspoon freshly ground
  black pepper
1 small red bell pepper,
  thinly sliced
2 ounces shredded
  part-skim mozzarella
  cheese (about ½ cup)
Basil leaves (optional)

1. Preheat broiler.

2. Split rolls lengthwise, cutting to, but not through, other side. Hollow out bottom halves of rolls. Arrange rolls, cut sides up, on a baking sheet. Broil 1½ minutes or until toasted. Set aside.

3. Heat a large skillet over medium-high heat. Add sausage to pan; cook 2 minutes or until lightly browned, stirring occasionally. Add onion and garlic; cook 1 minute. Add pasta sauce, black pepper, and bell pepper; bring to a boil. Reduce heat, and simmer 6 minutes or until bell pepper is crisp-tender.

4. Spoon about ¾ cup sausage mixture into rolls; sprinkle each serving with about 2 tablespoons cheese. Place on a baking sheet; broil 2 minutes or until cheese melts. Garnish with basil, if desired.

SERVES 4 (serving size: 1 hoagie)

CALORIES 309; FAT 7g (sat 4.4g, mono 0.9g, poly 0.1g); PROTEIN 20.7g; CARB 28.5g; FIBER 2.5g; CHOL 51mg; IRON 1.8mg; SODIUM 588mg; CALC 182mg

REAL MOM, REAL SMART

I sometimes let my toddler and pre-schooler stand on a step stool in front of the sink and "wash dishes" when I need to occupy them while I cook. It usually makes a big mess, but it's just water. And since I'm standing next to them chopping and cooking, I can still manage them a bit and make sure it doesn't get out of hand.

—Angie Tseng, Philadelphia, PA

Smashed Potatoes

Hands-on time: 5 min. Total time: 17 min.

I hardly ever made mashed potatoes because they just seemed too labor intensive. But these are shockingly easy, fast, and delicious. So now they're in frequent rotation, which I'm pretty sure makes my husband love me just a little bit more.

4 (6-ounce) baking potatoes, peeled and cut into 1-inch pieces
½ cup reduced-fat sour cream
½ cup 1% low-fat milk
2 tablespoons minced fresh chives
½ teaspoon salt
½ teaspoon freshly ground black pepper
Thinly sliced fresh chives (optional)

1. Place potato pieces in a 2-quart casserole. Cover, and microwave at HIGH 10 minutes. Let stand 2 minutes. Add sour cream and next 4 ingredients (through black pepper) to potatoes; mash with a potato masher to desired consistency. Garnish with chives, if desired.

SERVES 4 (serving size: 1 cup)

CALORIES 225; FAT 4.1g (sat 2.5g, mono 1.1g, poly 0.2g); PROTEIN 5.6g; CARB 42.6g; FIBER 2.8g; CHOL 13mg; IRON 0.8mg; SODIUM 333mg; CALC 78mg

CRAZY TRICK
that actually works!

Cook bacon in the oven instead of on the stovetop for less mess (and a lot less hands-on time). Line a baking sheet with foil, arrange your slices on the sheet, and bake at 425° for 18 to 20 minutes.

SLOW-COOKER
Applesauce

Hands-on time: 11 min. Total time: 4 hr. 11 min.

Like warm pie filling, this applesauce works as a light dessert or easy side dish with pork or chicken. And its heavenly scent wafting through your house is an extra bonus.

4 large Braeburn apples, peeled, cored, and quartered
2 tablespoons brown sugar
1/2 teaspoon ground cinnamon

1/8 teaspoon ground nutmeg
1/8 teaspoon salt
1/4 cup apple juice

1. Place apples in an electric slow cooker; sprinkle with brown sugar, cinnamon, nutmeg, and salt. Pour apple juice around apples. Cover and cook on HIGH for 4 hours.

2. Mash apple mixture with a potato masher or fork. Serve warm or at room temperature.

SERVES 6 (serving size: 1/2 cup)

CALORIES 81; **FAT** 17.6g (sat 0g, mono 0g, poly 0.1g); **PROTEIN** 0.4g; **CARB** 21.3g; **FIBER** 1.7g; **CHOL** 0mg; **IRON** 0.2mg; **SODIUM** 50mg; **CALC** 13mg

REAL MOM, REAL SMART

I have a kitchen cabinet reserved for pots, pans, and tools like measuring cups, potato masher, whisks, and spatulas that are safe for my 19-month-old to play with. He can only play with these while I'm cooking, so it feels special to him.

—Hannah Dinkel, Denver, CO

Chocolate Awesomeness Brownies

Hands-on time: 15 min. Total time: 57 min.

If you want to get your kids more involved in the kitchen, baking is a great place to start. And this recipe requires only 15 minutes of prep work. Henry gave the rich, fudgy brownies the perfect name.

3.4 ounces all-purpose flour (about ³/₄ cup)
1 cup granulated sugar
³/₄ cup unsweetened cocoa
¹/₂ cup packed brown sugar
¹/₂ teaspoon baking powder
¹/₄ teaspoon salt
1 cup bittersweet chocolate chunks, divided
¹/₃ cup fat-free milk
6 tablespoons butter, melted
1 teaspoon vanilla extract
2 large eggs, lightly beaten
¹/₂ cup chopped walnuts, divided
Cooking spray

1. Preheat oven to 350°.

2. Weigh or lightly spoon flour into dry measuring cups; level with a knife. Combine flour and next 5 ingredients (through salt) in a large bowl. Combine ¹/₂ cup chocolate and milk in a microwave-safe bowl; microwave at HIGH 1 minute, stirring after 30 seconds. Stir in butter, vanilla, and eggs. Add milk mixture, ¹/₂ cup chocolate, and ¹/₄ cup nuts to flour mixture; stir to combine.

3. Pour batter into a 9-inch square metal baking pan coated with cooking spray; sprinkle with ¹/₄ cup nuts. Bake at 350° for 30 minutes or until a wooden pick inserted in center comes out with moist crumbs clinging. Cool in pan on a wire rack. Cut into bars.

SERVES 20 (serving size: 1 bar)

CALORIES 286; **FAT** 9.1g (sat 4.2g, mono 2.2g, poly 1.7g); **PROTEIN** 2.8g; **CARB** 25.4g; **FIBER** 1.4g; **CHOL** 30mg; **IRON** 0.9mg; **SODIUM** 74mg; **CALC** 23mg

MEAT LOAF. AGAIN?

Busting Out of the Dinner Rut

One day when Henry was about 3 years old, he looked up at me with his big blue eyes and asked sweetly, "Mommy, are you ever going to take your hair out of that ponytail?" **I'm familiar with ruts—of both the stylistic and culinary varieties.** Just as I'm guilty of tying my hair back way too often, I'm guilty of going through jags of serving the same handful of dinners over and over (and over) again.

It's tempting to keep the same family favorites in heavy rotation, especially the ones you can practically pull together with one hand tied behind your back and that most family members will reliably eat. **But sticking with only those meals won't broaden your kids' horizons. And it also gets a little boring for everyone involved.** Just like my ponytail.

Put a new twist on an old favorite.

I wouldn't dream of taking meals like pot roast and tacos out of circulation. But there must be a way to give them a new spin. I asked Faith Durand, executive editor of the popular blog *The Kitchn*, for ideas.

Instead of tacos, make veggie tacos: Roast sweet potatoes or butternut squash with chili powder, and stuff tacos with these along with cheddar cheese and sour cream.

Instead of meat loaf, make surprise meat loaf: Bake meat loaf with a few peeled hard-cooked eggs inside or a streak of mashed potatoes.

Instead of chicken soup, make dumpling soup: In place of noodles or rice, make a basic dumpling dough out of flour, eggs, ricotta cheese, and water, and slip spoonfuls into simmering chicken soup. These dumplings are light yet chewy—a fun change from traditional egg noodles.

Instead of mashed potatoes, make golden mashed potatoes: Rutabaga (which looks intimidating but is actually easy to peel and prepare) steams and boils at the same rate as potatoes. Substituting rutabaga for half of the potatoes gives mashed potatoes a golden color and sweeter, richer taste.

Instead of pot roast, make mini pot roasts: Cut a chuck roast or brisket into 5-ounce pieces. They'll cook much faster in the oven or slow cooker. Serve with extra-small fingerling potatoes and baby carrots to go with the mini theme.

Eat out.

Strange advice in a cookbook, I know. But exposing your family to different cuisines may give you ideas for your own cooking and result in kids who appreciate all types of cuisines. Every couple of months, visit an authentic ethnic restaurant. While everyone may not fall in love with stuffed grape leaves or borscht, they may discover a new favorite. At the very least, you'll find some nugget of interest in the décor that will spawn interesting table trivia.

Be social.

The recipes in this chapter are all quirky in their own way: They contain unexpected ingredients (like beets in a burger or strawberries in a cookie) or call for an unconventional cooking method (like roasting kale leaves or grilling corn). If you're hungry for more, use these tips for finding dinner inspiration via social media.

Pinterest: Create boards like "Family Dinner Ideas" or "Try This" for pinning recipes as you're browsing the site or surfing the web.

Facebook: Follow your favorite food blogs, grocery chains, and cooking magazines, all of which regularly post recipes and ideas. Or put out a plea to your friends for their favorite recipes, and watch the comments roll in.

Twitter and Instagram: Search for hashtags—also known as key words—like #recipes, #chicken, or #healthyrecipes for up-to-the-minute recipes, pictures, and real-life testimonials.

GET A NEW GADGET.

A new kitchen tool can help you fight boredom and make it easier to try different recipes and cooking techniques. I've made more lemon-infused sauces and dressings since picking up an inexpensive citrus squeezer—and I would never have attempted microwave potato chips without a mandoline. Though these items may not make the cut for must-have gear (see page 41), they may spark some kitchen brilliance.

COOL NEW TOOL	JOB WELL DONE
IMMERSION BLENDER	Whip up smoothies; get lumps out of sauces; puree soups; blend salad dressings; and make hummus, mashed potatoes, and pesto.
MICROPLANE ZESTER	Add citrus zest to sweet and savory dishes to give them a bright, extra burst of flavor.
WOK	Stir-fry meats and vegetables quickly and with less oil than needed in a saucepan or skillet.
KITCHEN SHEARS	Cut fresh herbs or canned tomatoes without losing a finger.
BREAD MACHINE	Do the time-intensive work involved in making homemade pizza dough and breads.
MINI CHOPPER	Chop vegetables, fruit, garlic, herbs, and nuts, or grind graham crackers for a piecrust and bread for breadcrumbs.
SILICONE BAKING MATS	Bake sweet and savory dishes. Eliminates the need to coat baking sheets with cooking spray or line with parchment paper. Plus, they rinse clean with water.

SPEEDY Mahimahi with Glazed Pineapple

Hands-on time: 28 min. Total time: 28 min.

If you haven't tried it yet, mahimahi is a meaty fish that has a slightly sweet taste. (Pork chops work well with this recipe, too.) One peeled and cored fresh pineapple will yield just the right amount of fruit for this dish.

1 tablespoon butter
3 cups diced peeled
   pineapple
½ cup packed brown sugar
6 (6-ounce) mahimahi or
   other firm white fish fillets
   (about 1¼ inches thick)

½ teaspoon salt
¼ teaspoon freshly ground
   black pepper
Cooking spray
Sliced green onions
   (optional)

1. Melt butter in a large skillet over medium-high heat. Add pineapple; cook 7 minutes or until lightly browned, stirring occasionally. Sprinkle with brown sugar. Reduce heat to medium, and cook 2 minutes or until sugar melts and pineapple is glazed. Remove from heat; cool slightly.

2. Heat a grill pan over medium-high heat. Sprinkle both sides of fish with salt and pepper. Coat grill pan with cooking spray; add fish, and cook 6 minutes on each side or until fish flakes easily when tested with a fork. Place fish on a serving platter, and top with pineapple mixture. Garnish with green onions, if desired.

SERVES 6 (serving size: 1 fillet and about ½ cup pineapple mixture)

CALORIES 274; **FAT** 3.3g (sat 1.6g, mono 0.8g, poly 0.4g); **PROTEIN** 32g; **CARB** 29g; **FIBER** 1.2g; **CHOL** 129mg; **IRON** 2.3mg; **SODIUM** 369mg; **CALC** 52mg

CRAZY TRICK
that actually works!

If you usually plate food in the kitchen, start serving meals family style. It's a simple change, but it empowers kids—so they may be more receptive to trying new things because you've given them the choice. You're also teaching them to listen to their body's cues about hunger and fullness and to take only what they really want.

You can also use salmon packed in a foil pouch.

Salmon Cakes with Lemony Garlic Sauce

Hands-on time: 27 min. Total time: 42 min.

Here's a tip: Shaping the salmon mixture into balls, and letting them chill for 15 minutes helps them hold their shape while cooking, so don't skip that step.

1 tablespoon chopped fresh parsley

2 tablespoons canola mayonnaise

2 teaspoons fresh lemon juice

¼ teaspoon bottled minced garlic

¼ cup sliced green onions

3 tablespoons canola mayonnaise

2 tablespoons panko (Japanese breadcrumbs)

1 tablespoon chopped dill

2 teaspoons Dijon mustard

3 (6-ounce) cans skinless, boneless pink salmon in water, drained and squeezed dry

2 tablespoons canola oil

Lemon wedges

1. Combine first 4 ingredients in a small bowl; stir well. Cover, and chill sauce.

2. Combine onions and next 5 ingredients (through salmon) in a medium bowl; stir with a fork until well blended.

3. Divide salmon mixture into 8 equal portions, shaping each into a ball. Place balls on a plate; cover and refrigerate 15 minutes.

4. Shape each ball into a ½-inch-thick patty. Heat a large non-stick skillet over medium-high heat. Add 1 tablespoon oil to pan; swirl to coat. Place 4 patties in pan; cook 3 minutes on each side or until lightly browned. Repeat procedure with 1 tablespoon oil and remaining patties. Serve salmon cakes with sauce and lemon wedges.

SERVES 4 (serving size: 2 cakes and 1 tablespoon sauce)

CALORIES 253; **FAT** 19g (sat 2g, mono 7.3g, poly 3.7g); **PROTEIN** 17.9g; **CARB** 2.6g; **FIBER** 0.4g; **CHOL** 59mg; **IRON** 0.7mg; **SODIUM** 597mg; **CALC** 153mg

STOVETOP Pork Schnitzel

Hands-on time: 24 min. Total time: 24 min.

Think you've done everything with a package of pork chops? Pounded thin, dipped in milk, and dredged in breadcrumbs, humdrum chops suddenly become schnitzel! Serve the dill sauce on the side for dipping.

1/4 cup fat-free sour cream
1 tablespoon chopped dill
2 tablespoons low-fat
    buttermilk
3/4 teaspoon freshly ground
    black pepper, divided
5/8 teaspoon kosher salt,
    divided
1/4 cup fat-free milk
1 large egg, lightly beaten

3/4 cup dry breadcrumbs
2 tablespoons chopped
    fresh flat-leaf parsley
1/2 teaspoon garlic powder
4 (4-ounce) boneless
    center-cut loin pork chops,
    trimmed and pounded to
    1/8-inch thickness
2 tablespoons olive oil

1. Combine sour cream, dill, buttermilk, 1/4 teaspoon pepper, and 1/8 teaspoon salt in a bowl; set aside.

2. Combine milk and egg in a dish; stir with a whisk. In another dish, combine breadcrumbs, parsley, garlic powder, and 1/2 teaspoon pepper. Dip pork in milk mixture; sprinkle with 1/2 teaspoon salt. Dredge pork in breadcrumb mixture.

3. Heat a large nonstick skillet over medium-high heat. Add 1 tablespoon oil to pan; swirl to coat. Place 2 pork chops in pan. Cook 3 minutes on each side or until done. Repeat procedure with 1 tablespoon olive oil and remaining pork chops. Serve with sauce.

SERVES 4 (serving size: 1 schnitzel and 1 1/2 tablespoons sauce)

CALORIES 329; **FAT** 15.2g (sat 3.6g, mono 7.5g, poly 1.6g); **PROTEIN** 27.4g; **CARB** 19.3g; **FIBER** 1g; **CHOL** 115mg; **IRON** 1.1mg; **SODIUM** 540mg; **CALC** 80mg

Put a piece of plastic wrap or wax paper over the chops, and pound them thin so they'll cook more quickly.

Bacon Pierogi Bake

Hands-on time: 18 min. Total time: 38 min.

I grew up on my grandmother's homemade pierogies, hearty Polish dumplings stuffed with a potato filling. I've tried—and failed—to recreate them myself, but luckily some frozen kinds actually come close to the real deal (no disrespect, Grandma).

1 (16-ounce) package frozen potato and onion pierogies (such as Mrs. T's)
Cooking spray
2 center-cut bacon slices, chopped
2 garlic cloves, minced
3 ounces ⅓-less-fat cream cheese (about ⅓ cup)
½ cup fat-free, lower-sodium chicken broth
2 ounces shredded sharp cheddar cheese (about ½ cup)
¼ cup thinly diagonally sliced green onions
¼ cup chopped seeded plum tomato
½ teaspoon freshly ground black pepper

1. Preheat oven to 400°.

2. Arrange pierogies in an 11 x 7–inch glass or ceramic baking dish coated with cooking spray. Cook bacon in a saucepan over medium heat until crisp; remove from pan. Set aside.

3. Add garlic to drippings in pan, and cook 30 seconds, stirring constantly. Add cream cheese to pan, and cook 1 minute or until cream cheese begins to melt, stirring frequently. Gradually add chicken broth to pan, stirring with a whisk until smooth. Pour cream cheese mixture over pierogies. Top with cheddar cheese. Bake at 400° for 20 minutes or until bubbly and thoroughly heated. Remove from oven, and sprinkle with bacon, green onions, tomato, and pepper.

SERVES 4 (serving size: 3 pierogies and 2 tablespoons sauce)

CALORIES 303; FAT 12.8g (sat 6g, mono 4.3g, poly 0.4g); PROTEIN 12.1g; CARB 36.4g; FIBER 2.2g; CHOL 38mg; IRON 0.4mg; SODIUM 646mg; CALC 141mg

For a twist, bake in 4 (1-cup) shallow baking dishes for 10 minutes.

REAL MOM, REAL SMART

I take the ingredients from one recipe I know my family likes and mash it up with ingredients from another favorite and come up with some kind of Frankenstein meal. That's how we got "Taco Joes" and "Cheeseburger Pizza." It definitely breaks the monotony!

—Cheryll Robinson, Columbus, OH

Potato-Quinoa Croquettes

Hands-on time: 30 min. Total time: 45 min.

This makes a filling meal—no meat necessary.

1 (10-ounce) baking potato
2 cups water
1 cup uncooked quinoa, rinsed
½ teaspoon salt
4 teaspoons canola oil, divided
½ cup thinly sliced green onions
⅓ cup chopped fresh cilantro
1 jalapeño pepper, seeded and finely chopped
1 teaspoon ground cumin
½ teaspoon dried oregano
½ teaspoon black pepper
2 garlic cloves, minced
½ cup 1% low-fat cottage cheese
3 tablespoons shredded extra-sharp cheddar cheese
1 large egg, lightly beaten
1 cup panko (Japanese breadcrumbs)
10 teaspoons reduced-fat sour cream
1 cup pico de gallo

1. Preheat oven to 400°. Pierce potato with fork; bake at 400° for 1 hour or until tender. Cool, peel, and mash potato.

2. While potato bakes, bring 2 cups water to a boil in a saucepan; add quinoa and salt. Cook 15 minutes; drain.

3. Heat a large nonstick skillet over medium-high heat. Add 1 teaspoon oil; swirl. Add onions, cilantro, and jalapeño; sauté 1 minute. Add cumin, oregano, black pepper, and garlic; sauté 1 minute. Combine potato, quinoa, onion mixture, cottage cheese, and cheddar cheese in a bowl, stirring well. Let stand 5 minutes; stir in egg.

4. Shape potato mixture into 10 patties, and dredge in panko.

If the patties get too soft, chill them about 10 minutes so they'll firm up.

5. Heat 1½ teaspoons oil in pan over medium heat. Add 5 patties to pan; cook 2 minutes on each side or until golden brown. Keep warm. Repeat procedure with 1½ teaspoons oil and remaining patties. Top each patty with sour cream and pico de gallo.

SERVES 5 (serving size: 2 croquettes, 2 teaspoons sour cream, and about 3 tablespoons pico de gallo)

CALORIES 346; FAT 8.9g (sat 1.9g, mono 1.8g, poly 3.1g); PROTEIN 13g; CARB 53.6g; FIBER 4.1g; CHOL 48mg; IRON 3.8mg; SODIUM 450mg; CALC 85mg

Tofu-Broccoli Stir-Fry

Hands-on time: 31 min. Total time: 1 hr. 6 min.

Tofu is a great source of meatless protein, but use shrimp, chicken, or beef with this stir-fry if you prefer.

1 (14-ounce) package water-packed tofu, drained and cut crosswise into 6 slices
¾ cup water, divided
3 tablespoons natural-style creamy peanut butter
5 teaspoons brown sugar, divided
6 teaspoons lower-sodium soy sauce, divided
1 teaspoon Sriracha (hot chile sauce)
4 garlic cloves, chopped
5 teaspoons dark sesame oil, divided
2 cups thinly sliced carrot
1 cup (¼-inch-thick) strips red bell pepper
1 (12-ounce) package broccoli florets
½ cup sliced green onions
1 (8-ounce) can sliced water chestnuts, drained

1. Place tofu slices on several layers of paper towels; cover with additional paper towels and a flat plate. Weight the top of the plate with a heavy can. Let stand 30 minutes; discard paper towels. Cut tofu into ½-inch cubes.

2. Combine ¼ cup water, peanut butter, 3 teaspoons brown sugar, 1 teaspoon soy sauce, and Sriracha in a bowl. Set aside.

3. Combine 2 teaspoons brown sugar, 5 teaspoons soy sauce, and garlic in a small bowl, stirring with a whisk.

4. Heat a large nonstick skillet over medium-high heat. Add 3 teaspoons oil to pan; swirl to coat. Add tofu; stir-fry 7 minutes or until tofu is golden brown on all sides. Remove tofu from pan. Add 2 teaspoons oil to pan; swirl to coat. Add carrot, bell pepper, and broccoli to pan; stir-fry 3 minutes. Add ½ cup water; reduce heat to medium. Cover and simmer 5 minutes or until broccoli is crisp-tender. Stir in garlic mixture, tofu, green onions, and water chestnuts; stir-fry 2 minutes or until thoroughly heated. Serve with peanut sauce.

SERVES 4 (serving size: 1¾ cups tofu mixture and about 2½ tablespoons peanut sauce)

CALORIES 273; **FAT** 13.8g (sat 1.9g, mono 5.7g, poly 5.3g); **PROTEIN** 13.3g; **CARB** 26.7g; **FIBER** 6.4g; **CHOL** 0mg; **IRON** 3.2mg; **SODIUM** 415mg; **CALC** 109mg

Look for natural-style peanut butter that contains only peanuts and salt. Some versions labeled "natural" have added oil and sugar.

Beet and Brown Rice Sliders

Hands-on time: 32 min. Total time: 42 min.

16 slices sourdough bread
Cooking spray
1 cup cooled cooked whole-grain brown rice blend
3/4 cup grated cooked beet
1/2 cup panko (Japanese breadcrumbs)
6 tablespoons chopped walnuts, toasted
1/4 cup chopped parsley
2 tablespoons finely chopped shallots
1/2 teaspoon kosher salt
1/4 teaspoon freshly ground black pepper
2 tablespoons Dijon mustard
1 large egg
2 tablespoons olive oil
1 (3-ounce) log goat cheese, cut crosswise into 8 slices
1 cup watercress

1. Preheat broiler. Cut each bread slice into a 3-inch circle using a round cutter; reserve scraps for another use. Lightly coat bread rounds with cooking spray. Arrange rounds in a single layer on a baking sheet. Broil 2 minutes on each side or until toasted. Cool.

2. Place a baking sheet in oven, and reduce temperature to 400°.

3. Combine rice and next 7 ingredients (through black pepper) in a medium bowl. Combine mustard and egg, stirring well with a whisk. Add egg mixture to rice mixture; stir until well blended. Pack 1/3 cup rice mixture in a 2 1/2-inch round cookie cutter. Remove mixture from cookie cutter. Repeat procedure to form 8 patties.

4. Heat a large skillet over medium-high heat. Add 1 tablespoon oil to pan; swirl to coat. Add 4 patties to pan; cook 2 minutes. Carefully transfer patties, browned sides up, to preheated baking sheet. Repeat procedure with 1 tablespoon oil and remaining patties. Place pan in oven; bake at 400° for 9 minutes. Top each patty with 1 cheese slice; bake an additional minute or until cheese is soft and patties are set. Serve patties and watercress between toasted bread rounds.

SERVES 4 (serving size: 2 sliders)

CALORIES 405; **FAT** 21g (sat 5.3g, mono 7.6g, poly 6.5g); **PROTEIN** 14.4g; **CARB** 41.4g; **FIBER** 3.3g; **CHOL** 63mg; **IRON** 3.1mg; **SODIUM** 745mg; **CALC** 85mg

Eggplant Parmesan Sandwiches

Hands-on time: 18 min. Total time: 18 min.

Look for a slender eggplant so the slices fit the rolls.

8 (1.5-ounce) frozen artisan
  ciabatta rolls
1 cup panko (Japanese
  breadcrumbs)
1/3 cup all-purpose flour
2 large eggs, lightly beaten
1 medium eggplant, cut
  crosswise into 8 (1/2-inch-
  thick) slices
1/4 teaspoon salt

Cooking spray
16 large basil leaves
2 ounces fresh mozzarella
  cheese, shredded
8 teaspoons grated fresh
  Parmesan cheese
1 (24.5-ounce) jar organic
  pasta sauce (such as
  Amy's)

1. Heat ciabatta rolls according to package directions; cut rolls in half horizontally.

2. Preheat broiler.

3. Place panko, flour, and eggs in 3 separate shallow dishes. Sprinkle both sides of eggplant slices with salt. Dredge eggplant in flour. Dip in egg; dredge in panko. Place breaded eggplant slices on a baking sheet coated with cooking spray. Broil 3 minutes on each side or until browned. Place eggplant slices on a wire rack. Wipe baking sheet clean with a paper towel.

4. Place bottom halves of ciabatta rolls on baking sheet; top each with 1 basil leaf, 1 eggplant slice, another basil leaf, 1/4 ounce mozzarella cheese, and 1 teaspoon Parmesan cheese. Broil 1 minute or until cheese is lightly browned and bubbly.

5. Place marinara in a small microwave-safe bowl. Microwave at HIGH 1 minute or until hot. Spoon 1 tablespoon marinara over each sandwich; top with top halves of rolls.

SERVES 8 (serving size: 1 sandwich)

CALORIES 285; FAT 6.9g (sat 1.5g, mono 2.1g, poly 1.8g); PROTEIN 11.7g; CARB 44.2g; FIBER 6.1g; CHOL 53mg; IRON 1.9mg; SODIUM 824mg; CALC 88mg

SMART STRATEGY

Recreate a restaurant favorite. Do you hit certain restaurants over and over for one beloved dish? Try to replicate it at home—with a little online help. If it's a signature dish at a chain restaurant, chances are a blogger somewhere has done it already and posted a recipe. Otherwise, plug the name into a search engine, and see if you can find something close.

Roasted Brussels Sprouts and Apples

Hands-on time: 5 min. Total time: 30 min.

Leave the red apple skins on for a gorgeous color combination.

1 cup diced apple
1 pound Brussels sprouts, trimmed and quartered
¼ cup apple cider
4 teaspoons olive oil
2 teaspoons minced fresh thyme
½ teaspoon salt
¼ teaspoon freshly ground black pepper

1. Preheat oven to 375°.

2. Combine apple and Brussels sprouts in an 13 x 9–inch glass or ceramic baking dish. Add apple cider and remaining ingredients; toss well. Bake at 375° for 25 minutes or until sprouts are tender.

SERVES 4 (serving size: ¾ cup)

CALORIES 109; **FAT** 4.9g (sat 0.7g, mono 3.3g, poly 0.7g); **PROTEIN** 3.6g; **CARB** 15.8g; **FIBER** 4.7g; **CHOL** 0mg; **IRON** 1.6mg; **SODIUM** 321mg; **CALC** 47mg

REAL MOM, REAL SMART

I have about 90 recipes on cards in an envelope on the fridge, color-coded for chicken, fish, vegetarian, beef, pork, and turkey. I pick seven out each week. After the week is over, they go into a different envelope. I do this every week until the cards are gone. This way I know it'll be at least two months before a recipe is repeated.

—Toni Keith, Eliot, ME

EASY Garlic-Roasted Kale

Hands-on time: 11 min. Total time: 23 min.

I'm not going to guarantee that your kids will love kale after tasting this side dish. I will say that these crunchy, salty kale chips may just be your best chance of making that happen.

3½ teaspoons extra-virgin olive oil

¼ teaspoon kosher salt

1 garlic clove, thinly sliced

10 ounces chopped kale, stems removed

1 teaspoon sherry vinegar

1. Arrange oven racks in center and lower third of oven. Preheat oven to 425°. Place a large jelly-roll pan in oven for 5 minutes.

2. While pan heats, combine first 4 ingredients in a large bowl; toss to coat. Place kale mixture on hot pan, spreading with a silicone spatula to separate leaves. Bake at 425° for 7 minutes. Stir kale. Bake an additional 5 minutes or until edges of leaves are crisp and kale is tender.

3. Place kale in a large bowl. Drizzle with vinegar; toss gently. Serve immediately.

SERVES 4 (serving size: 1 cup)

CALORIES 72; **FAT** 4.7g (sat 0.7g, mono 3g, poly 0.8g); **PROTEIN** 2.3g; **CARB** 7.1g; **FIBER** 1.4g; **CHOL** 0mg; **IRON** 1.2mg; **SODIUM** 125mg; **CALC** 93mg

DINNERTIME SURVIVAL GUIDE TOP 5

TIPS FOR TRYING NEW FOODS

#1

KEEP FAVORITES ON THE TABLE. Potentially risky main course? Serve it with some much-loved mashed potatoes or a vegetable like corn or green beans that you know they reliably eat.

#2

ASK FOR REVIEWS. While trying out recipes for this book, I gave my children jobs they took seriously: recipe testers/reviewers. Knowing I valued their opinion encouraged them to try new foods and put their feedback into more words than "yum" or "yuck."

#3

GO SLOW. Intersperse new recipes with old standbys. Trying one new recipe a week is a nice place to start.

#4

GIVE IT A NAME. Research shows that people rate meals as tasting more delicious when there's a fancy name attached to them. So feel free to rebrand the Beet and Brown Rice Sliders as Pickalicious Burgers if it gets the job done.

#5

RESIST THE BACK-UP MEAL. Don't hop up from the table to make grilled cheese sandwiches if your new dish gets a thumbs-down. Let kids fill up on sides. Remember: one meal for the whole family!

White Chocolate, Strawberry, and Oatmeal Cookies

Hands-on time: 22 min. Total time: 35 min.

These are a sweet change of pace from regular chocolate chip cookies, and the whole batch is made with just half a stick of butter. This dough is heavy, so a stand or heavy-duty hand mixer is the perfect tool.

3.4 ounces all-purpose flour (about ¾ cup)
1 cup old-fashioned rolled oats
½ teaspoon baking soda
¼ teaspoon salt
¾ cup packed brown sugar
¼ cup butter, softened
1 teaspoon vanilla extract
1 large egg
¾ cup coarsely chopped dried strawberries
⅓ cup premium white chocolate chips (such as Ghirardelli)
Cooking spray

1. Preheat oven to 350°.

2. Weigh or lightly spoon flour into dry measuring cups; level with a knife. Combine flour, oats, baking soda, and salt; stir with a whisk. Place sugar and butter in the bowl of a stand mixer; beat at medium speed until well blended (about 3 minutes). Add vanilla and egg; beat well.

3. Gradually add flour mixture, beating until blended. Add strawberries and chocolate chips; beat at low speed just until blended.

4. Drop dough by tablespoonfuls 2 inches apart onto baking sheets coated with cooking spray. Bake at 350° for 12 minutes or until lightly browned. Remove from oven; cool 1 minute on pan. Remove cookies from pan; cool completely on wire racks.

MAKES 2 dozen (serving size: 1 cookie)

CALORIES 98; **FAT** 3.3g (sat 2.1g, mono 0.6g, poly 0.2g); **PROTEIN** 1.2g; **CARB** 16g; **FIBER** 0.6g; **CHOL** 14mg; **IRON** 0.5mg; **SODIUM** 73mg; **CALC** 11mg

Grilled Peaches with Honey Cream

Hands-on time: 15 min. Total time: 20 min.

Take "fruit for dessert" to a whole new level with these grilled peaches topped with a dollop of sweet cream.

2 tablespoons unsalted butter, melted

2 tablespoons honey, divided

¼ teaspoon ground cardamom

Dash of kosher salt

4 medium peaches, pitted and halved

Cooking spray

⅓ cup plain fat-free Greek yogurt

2½ tablespoons half-and-half

¼ teaspoon vanilla extract

1 cup raspberries

Mint leaves (optional)

1. Combine melted butter, 1 tablespoon honey, cardamom, and salt in a medium bowl. Add peaches, and toss to coat. Let stand 5 minutes.

2. Heat a grill pan over medium heat. Coat pan with cooking spray. Arrange peaches on grill pan; grill 2 minutes on each side or until grill marks appear.

3. Combine yogurt, half-and-half, vanilla, and 1 tablespoon honey in a small bowl; stir with a whisk. Serve with peaches and raspberries. Garnish with mint leaves, if desired.

SERVES 4 (serving size: ¼ cup raspberries, 2 tablespoons yogurt mixture, and 2 peach halves)

CALORIES 182; **FAT** 7.6g (sat 4.4g, mono 1.6g, poly 0.5g); **PROTEIN** 3.8g; **CARB** 27.9g; **FIBER** 4.2g; **CHOL** 19mg; **IRON** 0.7mg; **SODIUM** 43mg; **CALC** 42mg

No grill pan? Roast the peaches in the oven at 400° for about 20 minutes.

FRANKLY, I JUST DON'T FEEL LIKE IT

Easy Meals to Get It Done

There are nights when all the pieces are in place for making dinner. Our fridge is full, I've got a nice chunk of time, everyone is present and accounted for, and the kids are occupied with video games (I mean *math flashcards*). There's only one problem: I. Just. Don't. Want. To.

These are the nights I stand in front of the opened fridge, wishing the dinner fairy would descend or that I'd started teaching my kids to cook when they were toddlers.

To preserve my sanity, I usually build in nights for going out or ordering in. But to preserve our savings account, I try to limit that to just once a week. So instead of calling for take-out, I muddle through and pull together something simple. **And afterward, when we're clearing dishes from the table instead of greasy pizza boxes, I'm always, always glad I did.**

TRY THIS!

Embrace "leftover night."

That hodgepodge of leftover food in your fridge? Pure gold. It's also a win-win: You eliminate the pressure on yourself to cook a big meal (and avoid the cost and calories of restaurant food), and you keep everyone happy by letting them choose their meal from what's available. Leftover Night also has a little life lesson attached for kids: Use what you have and don't be wasteful. Here are three ways to give it a makeover.

Rebrand it: Never say *"leftovers."* My friend Lisa has "Smorg Night" every week (a term her kids *still* think is funny). She pulls out all the odds and ends from the fridge, and they stuff tortillas or make omelets. Alternate egos: Fend For Yourself Night, Fabulous Fridge Buffet, and Yo-Yo (You're On Your Own).

Relocate it: Have a picnic with your leftover food—in the yard or on the living room floor. The novel location will distract diners from the fact that you're serving a totally strange assortment of food for dinner.

Restyle it: Instead of just dumping all the plastic containers onto the counter, arrange leftovers on a nice serving platter. Chop up random leftovers, and toss with mixed greens. Whirl past-its-prime fruit into smoothies. A nice presentation just might mean more food eaten and fewer "I don't want this" gripes.

Cut yourself some slack.

You're officially not a bad parent if you resort to serving any of the following for dinner: peanut butter and jelly sandwiches, boxed macaroni and cheese, frozen pizza, grilled cheese sandwiches, pancakes from a mix, soup from a can, or fish sticks from a box.

As a dietitian, I'd rather see those meals reserved for "once in awhile." But I'd also rather see parents serving boxed mac and cheese for dinner instead of grabbing something in the drive-thru—especially if the boxed stuff is paired with healthy stuff you have on hand: a side of baby carrots and dip, a dish of edamame or other frozen veggie, a fruit smoothie, and a glass of milk. Those meals may not win you a James Beard Award, but they serve an important function: They get your family fed. And there's always tomorrow.

(Continued)

MAKE A LAST-DITCH EFFORT.

This chapter is full of recipes that you can pull together pretty quickly—and some (like the upgraded sandwiches) don't even feel like you're cooking. Most of the recipes don't require multiple pots and pans. Some don't require any pots at all. But if you need to simplify even more, here are four last-ditch meals.

LAST-DITCH MEAL	HOW TO MAKE IT HAPPEN
BAKED POTATO BAR	Microwave medium-sized baking potatoes, and set out assorted toppings like butter, sour cream, salsa, shredded cheese, left-over chili, bacon, green onions, avocado, and steamed broccoli.
EASY PIZZAS	Spread marinara sauce on flatbreads or pitas, sprinkle with cheese and favorite pizza toppings, and place under the broiler until hot and melty.
LOADED NACHOS	Arrange baked chips or sliced corn tortillas on a plate, sprinkle with cheese, canned beans, frozen corn, and any leftover beef or chicken from the fridge, and microwave until hot. Then top with salsa, avocado, olives, and green onions.
EGG SANDWICHES	Beat together several eggs, and cook them in a skillet. Cut into four pieces, and place on English muffins or toast with a slice of cheese and a piece of deli ham. Broil until cheese is melted.

Mediterranean Chicken Couscous

Hands-on time: 18 min. Total time: 23 min.

Hooray, it's a dinner that requires no pots or pans! Just use a glass measuring cup to heat the broth in the microwave, place uncooked couscous in the serving bowl, and then add the hot broth. Once everything else is stirred in, it's ready to serve.

1¼ cups fat-free, lower-sodium chicken broth

1 (5.6-ounce) package toasted pine nut couscous mix

3 cups chopped cooked chicken (about 1 rotisserie chicken)

¼ cup chopped fresh basil

1 teaspoon grated lemon rind

1½ tablespoons fresh lemon juice

¼ teaspoon freshly ground black pepper

1 pint grape tomatoes, halved

1 (4-ounce) package crumbled feta cheese

Basil leaves (optional)

1. Combine broth and seasoning packet from couscous mix in a large glass measuring cup. Microwave at HIGH 3 to 5 minutes or until broth begins to boil. Place uncooked couscous in a large bowl, and stir in broth mixture. Cover and let stand 5 minutes.

2. Fluff couscous with a fork; stir in chicken and next 6 ingredients (through cheese). Serve warm or cold. Garnish with basil leaves, if desired.

SERVES 8 (serving size: 1 cup)

CALORIES 212; FAT 6.8g (sat 3.1g, mono 1.9g, poly 1.1g); PROTEIN 21.3g; CARB 16.9g; FIBER 1.4g; CHOL 58mg; IRON 1.2mg; SODIUM 455mg; CALC 89mg

SMART STRATEGY

Start a dinner swap. When her kids were little, psychologist and parent coach Kathleen Cuneo, PhD, had a meal swap arrangement with her neighbor. On Mondays, she simply doubled whatever she was cooking, and gave it to her neighbor, who did the same for her family on Wednesdays. Occasionally they even ate the meals together. "It's hard to get dinner on the table every night, but we don't always have to do it alone," she says. "There are ways that we can support each other and build community while still providing our families with healthy meals."

EASY BBQ Chicken Kebabs

Hands-on time: 29 min. Total time: 29 min.

This chicken is just the right amount of spicy and cooks up in no time under the broiler. And I'm sure I'm not alone when I say: My kids absolutely love eating food off sticks.

1½ pounds chicken breast tenders (10 tenders)
4 teaspoons brown sugar
1 tablespoon paprika
½ teaspoon salt
½ teaspoon freshly ground black pepper
Cooking spray

1. Preheat broiler.

2. Thread chicken tenders onto 10 (4½- to 6-inch) skewers. Combine brown sugar, paprika, salt, and pepper in a bowl; stir well, and rub over tenders.

3. Place skewers on a broiler pan coated with cooking spray; broil 8 minutes on each side or until done, turning skewers occasionally.

SERVES 5 (serving size: 2 tenders)

CALORIES 175; FAT 3.9g (sat 0.8g, mono 1.2g, poly 0.7g); PROTEIN 29.1g; CARB 4.6g; FIBER 0.5g; CHOL 87mg; IRON 0.8mg; SODIUM 396mg; CALC 14mg

If using wooden skewers, soak them in water 30 minutes before using.

SMART STRATEGY

Work around a theme. Here's an approach used by a lot of meal-planning pros: Pick a broad theme for each night of the week, such as Mexican, Italian, Asian, sandwiches, and meatless. Then sit down with your family and brainstorm meal ideas together for each theme.

Vegetable Frittata

Hands-on time: 19 min. Total time: 29 min.

Frittatas are a great way to use up the leftover veggies hiding in your crisper drawer. Top each slice of this Italian egg dish with a spoonful of jarred marinara.

1½ tablespoons olive oil
1 cup diced zucchini
1 cup (1-inch) sliced
  asparagus
½ cup chopped red bell
  pepper
⅓ cup chopped onion
½ teaspoon salt, divided
¼ teaspoon freshly ground
  black pepper, divided

2 garlic cloves, minced
1 cup halved red or yellow
  grape tomatoes
9 large eggs
1 tablespoon chopped fresh
  basil
1 ounce finely shredded
  pecorino Romano cheese
  (about ¼ cup)

1. Heat a 10-inch ovenproof skillet over medium heat. Add oil to pan; swirl to coat. Add zucchini, asparagus, bell pepper, onion, ¼ teaspoon salt, ⅛ teaspoon black pepper, and garlic. Cook 6 minutes or until vegetables are tender, stirring occasionally. Add tomatoes; cook 4 minutes, stirring occasionally.

2. Combine ¼ teaspoon salt, ⅛ teaspoon black pepper, and eggs in a medium bowl, stirring well with a whisk. Add egg mixture and basil to pan, stirring gently to distribute vegetable mixture. Cover, reduce heat, and cook 10 minutes or until almost set in the center (do not stir).

3. Preheat broiler.

4. Sprinkle frittata with cheese. Broil 1 minute or until cheese melts. Invert frittata onto a platter; cut into 8 wedges. Serve immediately.

SERVES 4 (serving size: 2 wedges)

CALORIES 257; **FAT** 18g (sat 5.3g, mono 7.8g, poly 2.8g); **PROTEIN** 17g; **CARB** 7.5g; **FIBER** 2.1g; **CHOL** 424mg; **IRON** 3.1mg; **SODIUM** 752mg; **CALC** 128mg

BBQ Chicken–Blue Cheese Pizza

Hands-on time: 10 min. Total time: 18 min.

Using a packaged pizza crust and bottled barbecue sauce, this twist on traditional pizza requires only 10 minutes of your undivided attention. You'll love the sharp, salty flavor of blue cheese here—but if you're not sure your kids will, sprinkle mozzarella on half just in case.

1 (8-ounce) prebaked thin pizza crust (such as Mama Mary's)

⅓ cup barbecue sauce

1½ cups shredded skinless, boneless rotisserie chicken breast

½ cup vertically sliced red onion

½ cup coarsely chopped yellow bell pepper

2 ounces crumbled blue cheese (about ½ cup)

2 plum tomatoes, thinly sliced (about ¼ pound)

1. Preheat oven to 500°.

2. Place pizza crust on a baking sheet. Spread sauce over crust, leaving a ½-inch border. Top with chicken and remaining ingredients. Bake at 500° for 8 minutes or until cheese melts and crust is crisp. Cut into 12 wedges.

SERVES 6 (serving size: 2 wedges)

CALORIES 252; FAT 8.5g (sat 3.1g, mono 2.2g, poly 2.7g); PROTEIN 16.7g; CARB 27.4g; FIBER 1.8g; CHOL 38mg; IRON 1.6mg; SODIUM 494mg; CALC 92mg

CRAZY TRICK
that actually works!

If you don't want to turn on your oven, throw your pizza onto the grill. Use either homemade or store-bought dough (or a pre-baked shell, as in this recipe), and cook it on low heat. I promise, it won't slip through the grates!

DINNERTIME SURVIVAL GUIDE TOP 5

TIPS FOR DINING OUT

#1

CHOOSE WISELY: Kids are loud. And eating out isn't fun if you're constantly shushing yours. Pick a family-friendly place, and save fine dining for date nights.

#2

DELAY THE DRINKS: If my kids order a beverage beyond water, I ask the server to bring it out with the meal so they don't guzzle it down and fill up before the food arrives. We all sip water while we wait.

#3

STAY CONSISTENT: I don't let my kids lie under the table at home or run through the house with their napkin around their neck superhero style, so ditto for restaurants. You don't want to be *those* parents with *that* kid, right?

#4

DON'T MICROMANAGE: Give older kids some guidelines but let them make decisions, too. I make sure mine know that ordering from the "real" menu (not the child's menu) is an impressive "big-kid" move.

#5

BE REALISTIC: Grown-ups love lingering over multiple courses and drinks. Your children probably don't. Be efficient with your time—and understanding when your kids get antsy.

Black Bean Soup

Hands-on time: 20 min. Total time: 36 min.

Using canned beans and ready-made salsa stream-lines the prep on this simple Southwestern-style soup. Pick your favorite toppings to add color and flavor: Shredded cheddar, crumbled tortilla chips, green onions, and sour cream work well. Half the soup is pureed to give a mix of chunky and creamy textures.

1 teaspoon olive oil
1/4 cup chopped onion
1 garlic clove, minced
2 cups organic vegetable broth
1/2 teaspoon Spanish smoked paprika
1/4 teaspoon ground cumin
1/4 teaspoon dried oregano
2 (15-ounce) cans unsalted black beans, rinsed and drained
1/2 cup refrigerated fresh salsa
3/8 teaspoon salt
1 (4.5-ounce) can chopped green chiles, drained
1 diced peeled avocado (optional)
1 tomato, chopped (optional)
Chopped fresh cilantro (optional)

Slice the avocado lengthwise all around the pit, and twist the top half to open.

1. Heat a large saucepan over medium-high heat. Add oil to pan; swirl to coat. Add onion and garlic; sauté 3 minutes or until tender. Add broth and next 4 ingredients (through beans); bring to a boil. Cover, reduce heat, and simmer 10 minutes.

2. Place half of bean mixture in a blender. Remove center piece of blender lid (to allow steam to escape); secure blender lid on blender. Place a clean towel over opening in blender lid (to avoid splatters). Blend until smooth. Add pureed soup to remaining soup in pan. Stir in salsa, salt, and green chiles; cook over medium heat 3 minutes or until thoroughly heated.

3. Ladle soup into each of 4 bowls; top with avocado, tomato, and cilantro, if desired.

SERVES 4 (serving size: 1 cup)

CALORIES 182; **FAT** 1.2g (sat 0.8g, mono 0.8g, poly 0.2g); **PROTEIN** 10.6g; **CARB** 32.3g; **FIBER** 9.4g; **CHOL** 0mg; **IRON** 2.9mg; **SODIUM** 1005mg; **CALC** 95mg

Almond-Rosemary Chicken Salad Sandwiches

Hands-on time: 8 min. Total time: 8 min.

*Have leftover chicken from last night? Fresh rosemary
and smoked almonds add elegance to this salad, which
has been called "astoundingly delicious" and "the best
chicken salad ever" by bowled-over reviewers.*

3 cups chopped roasted
   skinless, boneless chicken
   breast (about ¾ pound)
⅓ cup chopped green
   onions
¼ cup chopped smoked
   almonds
¼ cup plain fat-free yogurt
¼ cup light mayonnaise

1 teaspoon chopped fresh
   rosemary
1 teaspoon Dijon mustard
⅛ teaspoon salt
⅛ teaspoon freshly ground
   black pepper
10 slices whole-grain bread
5 green leaf lettuce leaves

1. Combine first 9 ingredients, stirring well. Spread about ⅔ cup
chicken mixture over each of 5 bread slices; top with lettuce leaves
and remaining bread slices. Cut sandwiches in half.

SERVES 5 (serving size: 1 sandwich)

CALORIES 360; **FAT** 11.6g (sat 2.1g, mono 3.5g, poly 1.8g); **PROTEIN** 33.6g; **CARB** 29.9g;
FIBER 4.4g; **CHOL** 76mg; **IRON** 2.9mg; **SODIUM** 529mg; **CALC** 104mg

EASY Turkey, Apple, and Swiss Melts

Hands-on time: 19 min. Total time: 19 min.

Adding slices of crisp apple and an easy honey mustard spread works wonders on a regular turkey sandwich. You can use your favorite red apple or pear here instead.

1 tablespoon Dijon mustard
1 tablespoon honey
8 (1-ounce) slices whole-wheat bread
4 (1-ounce) slices Swiss cheese
20 thin Granny Smith apple slices (about 1 small)
8 ounces thinly sliced lower-sodium deli turkey breast
Cooking spray

1. Combine mustard and honey in a small bowl. Spread 1 side of each of 4 bread slices with 1½ teaspoons mustard mixture. Place 1 cheese slice on dressed side of bread slices; top each with 5 apple slices and 2 ounces turkey. Top sandwiches with remaining bread slices. Coat both sides of sandwiches with cooking spray. Heat a large nonstick skillet over medium-high heat. Add sandwiches to pan. Cook 2 minutes on each side or until bread is browned and cheese melts.

SERVES 4 (serving size: 1 sandwich)

CALORIES 350; **FAT** 10.9g (sat 5.5g, mono 3g, poly 0.6g); **PROTEIN** 27.2g; **CARB** 34.5g; **FIBER** 4.3g; **CHOL** 46mg; **IRON** 1.9mg; **SODIUM** 758mg; **CALC** 287mg

REAL MOM, REAL SMART

We sometimes do Snack Dinner—cooked bow tie pasta, cherry tomatoes, fresh fruit, edamame in the pod, raw veggies, and glasses of milk. The kids love this. They can eat as much or as little of any of the things they want.

—Tina Hennessey, State College, PA

Prosciutto, Pear, and Blue Cheese Sandwiches

Hands-on time: 20 min. Total time: 20 min.

This sounds and tastes like a specialty sandwich from an upscale deli—and you will love the combination of salty prosciutto, creamy blue cheese, and crispy sweet pears.

8 slices multigrain bread
1 tablespoon butter, softened
3 cups arugula
1 medium shallot, thinly sliced
1 tablespoon extra-virgin olive oil
2 teaspoons red wine vinegar
⅛ teaspoon freshly ground black pepper
2 ounces thinly sliced prosciutto
1 ripe pear, cored and thinly sliced
2 ounces blue cheese, sliced

Splurge on prosciutto if you can. Otherwise, use good deli ham sliced thin.

1. Preheat broiler.

2. Arrange bread in a single layer on a baking sheet; broil 3 minutes or until toasted. Turn bread slices over; spread butter evenly over bread slices. Broil an additional 2 minutes or until toasted.

3. Combine arugula and shallots in a medium bowl. Drizzle arugula mixture with oil and vinegar; sprinkle with pepper. Toss well to coat. Divide arugula mixture evenly among 4 bread slices, buttered side up; top evenly with prosciutto. Divide pear slices and cheese evenly among sandwiches; top each sandwich with 1 bread slice, buttered side down.

SERVES 4 (serving size: 1 sandwich)

CALORIES 324; **FAT** 13.8g (sat 5.4g, mono 5g, poly 0.8g); **PROTEIN** 15g; **CARB** 36.4g; FIBER 9.7g; **CHOL** 26mg; **IRON** 2.1mg; **SODIUM** 706mg; **CALC** 408mg

Grilled Tomato and Brie Sandwiches

Hands-on time: 20 min. Total time: 20 min.

There's something about Brie that makes a dish feel fancier than it really is. And here's a bright idea: Put older kids to work making these sandwiches while you sit down with a nice glass of wine.

2 tablespoons canola mayonnaise
1 garlic clove, minced
8 (0.9-ounce) slices 100% whole-grain bread (about ¼ inch thick)
3.5 ounces Brie cheese, thinly sliced

1⅓ cups baby spinach
8 (¼-inch-thick) slices beefsteak tomato
4 center-cut bacon slices, cooked and halved
Cooking spray

1. Combine mayonnaise and garlic; spread mixture evenly on 1 side of each of 4 bread slices. Top each with about ¾ ounce cheese, ⅓ cup spinach, 2 tomato slices, and 2 half-slices bacon. Top with remaining bread slices.

2. Heat a large grill pan over medium-high heat. Coat pan with cooking spray. Place sandwiches on pan; grill 2 minutes on each side or until lightly toasted and cheese melts.

SERVES 4 (serving size: 1 sandwich)

CALORIES 274; **FAT** 12.9g (sat 5.3g, mono 4.3g, poly 2.1g); **PROTEIN** 14.6g; **CARB** 24.9g; **FIBER** 4.7g; **CHOL** 30mg; **IRON** 1.8mg; **SODIUM** 517mg; **CALC** 109mg

SMART STRATEGY

Pick wholesome nuggets. Got a box of chicken nuggets on standby in the freezer? No judgment from me. But consider a few things when buying them: Look for "made with white meat" on the package. With any product, look for a shorter ingredient list (if you can't pronounce most of it, chances are it contains lots of preservatives and fillers). If you'd like to avoid chicken raised with antibiotics, choose an organic brand.

In the drive-thru, get the smallest size you can: Even a six-piece order has a quarter of your kid's daily limit for sodium and almost a third of their daily need for fat. (That's more than a regular fast-food hamburger!).

Mexican Cobb Salad

Hands-on time: 23 min. Total time: 23 min.

If you're a parent, you probably have a bottle of ranch dressing in your house. Here, it's dressed up with some salsa verde, cilantro, lime juice, and a touch of black pepper to top this hearty salad. You can always line up the ingredients buffet-style, and let everyone customize their plate of greens.

8 cups bagged 5-lettuce mixed salad greens

1 cup halved grape tomatoes

1 cup diced red onion

1 cup diced peeled jicama or carrot

1 cup diced green bell pepper

1 cup fresh corn kernels (about 2 ears)

1 cup diced peeled avocado

1 cup thinly sliced radishes

1 (15-ounce) can unsalted black beans, rinsed and drained

4 ounces shredded reduced-fat colby-Jack or reduced-fat Monterey Jack cheese (about 1 cup)

1 cup coarsely crushed baked tortilla chips

1/2 cup light ranch dressing

1/4 cup salsa verde

1 tablespoon chopped fresh cilantro

2 teaspoons fresh lime juice

1/4 teaspoon freshly ground black pepper

1. Place 1⅓ cups salad greens on each of 6 plates. Arrange about 2½ tablespoons tomatoes, about 2½ tablespoons onion, about 2½ tablespoons jicama, about 2½ tablespoons bell pepper, about 2½ tablespoons corn, about 2½ tablespoons avocado, about 2½ tablespoons radishes, and about ¼ cup beans in individual rows over each plate of salad greens. Sprinkle about 2½ tablespoons cheese and about 2½ tablespoons crushed chips over each salad.

2. Combine ranch dressing, salsa verde, cilantro, lime juice, and black pepper in a small bowl; stir well. Drizzle 2 tablespoons dressing over each salad.

SERVES 6 (serving size: 1 salad)

CALORIES 306; FAT 14g (sat 4g, mono 5.3g, poly 3.1g); PROTEIN 11.5g; CARB 38.2g; FIBER 8.9g; CHOL 20mg; IRON 2.1mg; SODIUM 683mg; CALC 201mg

REAL MOM, REAL SMART

I use a Lazy Susan in the middle of the kitchen table and declare "make your own" night, like Pasta Night with sauces or Taco Night with bowls of toppings. It's interactive and gives us all a chance to experiment with our food. The bonus is that it gets the whole family involved in dinner prep.

—Jess Jordan Pedersen, blogger, bemamabewell.com

Sweet and Hot Carrot Salad with Cranberries

Hands-on time: 10 min. Total time: 40 min.

Use fresh carrots for this fun salad—they're sweeter and have a better texture than the pre-shredded kind. A food processor fitted with a shredding blade gets the job done quickly.

1/4 cup extra-virgin olive oil

2 tablespoons fresh lime juice

1/2 teaspoon sambal oelek (ground fresh chile paste)

4 cups shredded carrot (about 1 pound)

1/3 cup golden raisins

1/3 cup sweetened dried cranberries

3/8 teaspoon kosher salt

2 1/2 tablespoons chopped fresh cilantro

1 1/2 tablespoons minced fresh mint

1. Combine first 3 ingredients in a large bowl, stirring with a whisk. Add carrot, raisins, cranberries, and salt; toss to coat. Let stand 30 minutes. Stir in cilantro and mint just before serving.

SERVES 8 (serving size: 1/2 cup)

CALORIES 122; **FAT** 7.2g (sat 1g, mono 5.4g, poly 0.7g); **PROTEIN** 0.8g; **CARB** 14.8g; **FIBER** 2.2g; **CHOL** 0mg; **IRON** 0.3mg; **SODIUM** 148mg; **CALC** 24mg

SPEEDY Berry and Banana Smoothies

Hands-on time: 10 min. Total time: 10 min.

A satisfying source of protein and fiber, this smoothie pairs well with low-maintenance dinners of pancakes or PB&Js. Use the berries your family likes best, like blueberries or raspberries. The orange juice and fruit give this smoothie a lot of sweetness, so feel free to leave out the honey.

1¾ cups plain fat-free
   Greek yogurt
½ cup fresh orange juice
   (about 1 large orange)

1 tablespoon honey
1 cup hulled strawberries
1 cup blackberries
1 frozen sliced banana

1. Place all ingredients in a blender; process until smooth.

SERVES 4 (serving size: about 1 cup)

CALORIES 138; **FAT** 0.4g (sat 0g, mono 0g, poly 0.2g); **PROTEIN** 9.8g; **CARB** 25.3g; **FIBER** 3.4g; **CHOL** 0mg; **IRON** 0.6mg; **SODIUM** 38mg; **CALC** 86mg

REAL MOM, REAL SMART

When I don't have the will or the way to make dinner? Eggs. Eggs. Eggs. Picky kids can have them scrambled or fried on a roll from the freezer, and moms and dads can douse them with hot sauce. Works every time.

—Rebecca Fishkin, Lawrenceville, NJ

NUTRITIONAL INFORMATION

How to Use It and Why

Glance at the end of any *Cooking Light* recipe, and you'll see how committed we are to helping you make the best of today's light cooking. With chefs, registered dietitians, home economists, and a computer system that analyzes every ingredient we use, *Cooking Light* gives you authoritative dietary detail like no other magazine. We go to such lengths so you can see how our recipes fit into your healthful eating plan. If you're trying to lose weight, the calorie and fat figures will probably help most. But if you're keeping a close eye on the sodium, cholesterol, and saturated fat in your diet, we provide those numbers, too. And because many women don't get enough iron or calcium, we can help there, as well. Finally, there's a fiber analysis for those of us who don't get enough roughage.

Here's a helpful guide to put our nutritional analysis numbers into perspective. Remember, one size doesn't fit all, so take your lifestyle, age, and circumstances into consideration when determining your nutrition needs. For example, pregnant or breast-feeding women need more protein, calories, and calcium. And women older than 50 need 1,200mg of calcium daily, 200mg more than the amount recommended for younger women.

In Our Nutritional Analysis, We Use These Abbreviations

sat saturated fat	CARB carbohydrates	g gram
mono monounsaturated fat	CHOL cholesterol	mg milligram
poly polyunsaturated fat	CALC calcium	

Daily Nutrition Guide

	Women ages 25 to 50	Women over 50	Men ages 24 to 50	Men over 50
Calories	2,000	2,000 or less	2,700	2,500
Protein	50g	50g or less	63g	60g
Fat	65g or less	65g or less	88g or less	83g or less
Saturated Fat	20g or less	20g or less	27g or less	25g or less
Carbohydrates	304g	304g	410g	375g
Fiber	25g to 35g	25g to 35g	25g to 35g	25g to 35g
Cholesterol	300mg or less	300mg or less	300mg or less	300mg or less
Iron	18mg	8mg	8mg	8mg
Sodium	2,300mg or less	1,500mg or less	2,300mg or less	1,500mg or less
Calcium	1,000mg	1,200mg	1,000mg	1,000mg

The nutritional values used in our calculations either come from The Food Processor, Version 10.4 (ESHA Research), or are provided by food manufacturers.

METRIC EQUIVALENTS

The information in the following charts is provided to help cooks outside the United States successfully use the recipes in this book. All equivalents are approximate.

Cooking/Oven Temperatures

	Fahrenheit	Celsius	Gas Mark
Freeze Water	32° F	0° C	
Room Temp.	68° F	20° C	
Boil Water	212° F	100° C	
Bake	325° F	160° C	3
	350° F	180° C	4
	375° F	190° C	5
	400° F	200° C	6
	425° F	220° C	7
	450° F	230° C	8
Broil			Grill

Liquid Ingredients by Volume

¼ tsp	=					1 ml		
½ tsp	=					2 ml		
1 tsp	=					5 ml		
3 tsp	=	1 Tbsp	=	½ fl oz	=	15 ml		
2 Tbsp	=	⅛ cup	=	1 fl oz	=	30 ml		
4 Tbsp	=	¼ cup	=	2 fl oz	=	60 ml		
5⅓ Tbsp	=	⅓ cup	=	3 fl oz	=	80 ml		
8 Tbsp	=	½ cup	=	4 fl oz	=	120 ml		
10⅔ Tbsp	=	⅔ cup	=	5 fl oz	=	160 ml		
12 Tbsp	=	¾ cup	=	6 fl oz	=	180 ml		
16 Tbsp	=	1 cup	=	8 fl oz	=	240 ml		
1 pt	=	2 cups	=	16 fl oz	=	480 ml		
1 qt	=	4 cups	=	32 fl oz	=	960 ml		
				33 fl oz	=	1000 ml	=	1 l

Dry Ingredients by Weight

(To convert ounces to grams, multiply the number of ounces by 30.)

1 oz	=	¹⁄₁₆ lb	=	30 g
4 oz	=	¼ lb	=	120 g
8 oz	=	½ lb	=	240 g
12 oz	=	¾ lb	=	360 g
16 oz	=	1 lb	=	480 g

Length

(To convert inches to centimeters, multiply the number of inches by 2.5.)

1 in	=				2.5 cm		
6 in	=	½ ft		=	15 cm		
12 in	=	1 ft		=	30 cm		
36 in	=	3 ft	=	1 yd	90 cm		
40 in	=				100 cm	=	1 m

Equivalents for Different Types of Ingredients

Standard Cup	Fine Powder (ex. flour)	Grain (ex. rice)	Granular (ex. sugar)	Liquid Solids (ex. butter)	Liquid (ex. milk)
1	140 g	150 g	190 g	200 g	240 ml
¾	105 g	113 g	143 g	150 g	180 ml
⅔	93 g	100 g	125 g	133 g	160 ml
½	70 g	75 g	95 g	100 g	120 ml
⅓	47 g	50 g	63 g	67 g	80 ml
¼	35 g	38 g	48 g	50 g	60 ml
⅛	18 g	19 g	24 g	25 g	30 ml

INDEX

Spinach *(continued)*

©2014 by Time Home Entertainment Inc.
135 West 50th Street, New York, NY 10020

ISBN-13: 978-0-8487-4242-3
ISBN-10: 0-8487-4242-7
Library of Congress Control Number: 2013949549

Printed in the United States of America
First Printing 2014

Oxmoor House

Vice President, Brand Publishing: Laura Sappington
Editorial Director: Leah McLaughlin
Creative Director: Felicity Keane
Brand Manager: Michelle Turner Aycock
Senior Editor: Andrea C. Kirkland, MS, RD
Managing Editor: Elizabeth Tyler Austin
Assistant Managing Editor: Jeanne de Lathouder

Cooking Light Dinnertime Survival Guide

Editor: Rachel Quinlivan West, RD
Art Director: Christopher Rhoads
Project Editor: Lacie Pinyan
Assistant Designer: Allison Sperando Potter
Junior Designer: Maribeth Jones
Executive Food Director: Grace Parisi
Assistant Test Kitchen Manager: Alyson Moreland Haynes
Recipe Developers and Testers: Wendy Ball, RD; Tamara Goldis, RD; Stefanie Maloney; Callie Nash; Karen Rankin; Leah Van Deren
Food Stylists: Victoria E. Cox, Margaret Monroe Dickey, Catherine Crowell Steele
Photography Director: Jim Bathie
Senior Photographer: Hélène Dujardin
Senior Photo Stylist: Kay E. Clarke
Photo Stylist: Mindi Shapiro Levine
Assistant Photo Stylist: Mary Louise Menendez
Production Managers: Theresa Beste-Farley, Tamara Nall Wilder

Contributors

Author: Sally Kuzemchak, MS, RD
Editor: Elizabeth Taliaferro
Designer: Howard Grossman
Recipe Developer and Tester: Jan Smith
Copy Editors: Jacqueline Giovanelli, Dolores Hydock
Nutrition Analysis: Carolyn Land Williams, PhD, RD
Indexer: Mary Ann Laurens

Fellows: Ali Carruba, Frances Higginbotham, Elizabeth Laseter, Amy Pinney, Madison Taylor Pozzo, Deanna Sakal, April Smitherman, Megan Thompson, Tonya West
Food Stylist: Erica Hopper
Photographer: Lauryn Byrdy
Photo Stylists: Mary Clayton Carl, Lydia Degaris-Purcell, Cydney Schaumburg, Leslie Simpson
Wardrobe Stylist: Lily Schlosser
Hair & Make Up Stylist: Katrina Rutherford

Cooking Light

Editor: Scott Mowbray
Creative Director: Dimity Jones
Executive Managing Editor: Phillip Rhodes
Executive Editor, Food: Ann Taylor Pittman
Executive Editor, Digital: Allison Long Lowery
Special Publications Editor: Mary Simpson Creel, MS, RD
Senior Food Editor: Timothy Q. Cebula
Senior Editor: Cindy Hatcher
Assistant Editor, Nutrition: Sidney Fry, MS, RD
Assistant Editors: Kimberly Holland, Hannah Klinger
Test Kitchen Manager: Tiffany Vickers Davis
Recipe Testers and Developers: Robin Bashinsky, Adam Hickman, Deb Wise
Art Directors: Rachel Cardina Lasserre, Sheri Wilson
Senior Designer: Anna Bird
Designer: Hagen Stegall
Assistant Designer: Nicole Gerrity
Tablet Designer: Daniel Boone
Photo Director: Julie Claire
Assistant Photo Editor: Amy Delaune
Senior Photographer: Randy Mayor
Senior Prop Stylist: Cindy Barr
Assistant Prop Stylist: Lindsey Lower
Chief Food Stylist: Kellie Gerber Kelley
Food Styling Assistant: Blakeslee Giles
Production Director: Liz Rhoades
Production Editor: Hazel R. Eddins
Production Coordinator: Caitlin Murphree Miller
Copy Director: Susan Roberts McWilliams
Copy Editor: Kate Johnson
Research Editor: Michelle Gibson Daniels
Administrative Coordinator: Carol D. Johnson
CookingLight.com Editor: Mallory Daugherty Brasseale
CookingLight.com Assistant Editor/Producer: Michelle Klug

Time Home Entertainment Inc.

Publisher: Jim Childs
Vice President, Brand & Digital Strategy: Steven Sandonato
Executive Director, Marketing Services: Carol Pittard
Executive Director, Retail & Special Sales: Tom Mifsud
Director, Bookazine Development & Marketing: Laura Adam
Executive Publishing Director: Joy Butts
Associate Publishing Director: Megan Pearlman
Finance Director: Glenn Buonocore
Associate General Counsel: Helen Wan

ACKNOWLEDGEMENTS

I am so very grateful for my editors, Elizabeth Taliaferro and Rachel West, who made this process a joy; for my agent, Carole Bidnick, who was in my corner from the very first phone call and gave me an important pep talk right when I needed it; and for the team at Oxmoor House for their hard work—thank you for asking me to be part of the amazing *Cooking Light* brand. I am honored. Thanks also to Lauryn Byrdy and crew for making me look a lot less frazzled than I usually am!

Big thanks to my blogger friends Brianne DeRosa, Katie Morford, Danielle Omar, and Brenda Thompson who allowed me to adapt their recipes; to Faith Durand, Grace Freedman, Danielle Omar, and Shelley Young for their expert advice; and to all the moms who provided the "Real Mom" tips sprinkled throughout this book. I learned so much from all of you.

To my friends who provided recipe testing, tasting, and general wisdom: Laura Kraus, Courtney Phillips, Karina Brown, Colby Srsic, Janelle Tucker, Janellen Evans, and especially to Lisa Evans, who regularly swoops in and saves my day.

Thank you to the wonderful community of women on my Real Mom Nutrition Facebook page, who share their triumphs and tragedies when it comes to cooking dinner and feeding kids. Thank you for the inspiration and the company. I love spending time with you every day.

Thank you to my mom and dad, who are always in my cheering section no matter what.

To my husband Joel: Without you, my dear man, there would be no Real Mom Nutrition. Thank you for learning to like asparagus for the sake of our kids, thanking me for every meal I make, and most importantly, for always washing the dishes.

Finally, to the two little boys at my dinner table every night, Henry and Sam. Thank you for bringing so much love and happy noise into my life and teaching me just how much family dinner really matters. I'd cook dinner for you guys any night of the week. Oh that's right, I already do.